T0035502

THE MINE WARS

THE BLOODY FIGHT FOR WORKERS' RIGHTS IN THE WEST VIRGINIA COALFIELDS

THE
MINE WARS

THE BLOODY FIGHT FOR WORKERS' RIGHTS
IN THE WEST VIRGINIA COALFIELDS

STEVE WATKINS

BLOOMSBURY
CHILDREN'S BOOKS
NEW YORK LONDON OXFORD NEW DELHI SYDNEY

BLOOMSBURY CHILDREN'S BOOKS
Bloomsbury Publishing Inc., part of Bloomsbury Publishing Plc
1385 Broadway, New York, NY 10018

BLOOMSBURY, BLOOMSBURY CHILDREN'S BOOKS, and the Diana logo
are trademarks of Bloomsbury Publishing Plc

First published in the United States of America in May 2024
by Bloomsbury Children's Books

Text copyright © 2024 by Steve Watkins

All rights reserved. No part of this publication may be reproduced or transmitted in any form or by
any means, electronic or mechanical, including photocopying, recording, or any information storage
or retrieval system, without prior permission in writing from the publisher.

Bloomsbury books may be purchased for business or promotional use. For information on bulk
purchases please contact Macmillan Corporate and Premium Sales Department at
specialmarkets@macmillan.com

Library of Congress Cataloging-in-Publication Data
Names: Watkins, Steve, author.
Title: The mine wars : the bloody fight for workers' rights in the
West Virginia coalfields / by Steve Watkins.
Description: New York : Bloomsbury, 2024. | Includes bibliographical references.
Summary: The true story of the West Virginia coal miners who ignited
the largest labor uprising in American history.
Identifiers: LCCN 2024002829 (print) | LCCN 2024002830 (e-book)
ISBN 978-1-5476-1218-5 (hardcover) • ISBN 978-1-5476-1219-2 (e-book)
Subjects: LCSH: West Virginia Mine Wars, W. Va., 1897–1921—Juvenile literature. |
Strikes and lockouts—Coal mining—West Virginia—History—Juvenile literature. |
Coal miners—Labor unions—West Virginia—History—Juvenile literature. |
Coal mines and mining—West Virginia—History—Juvenile literature.
Classification: LCC HD5325.M615 W37 2024 (print) | LCC HD5325.M615 (e-book) |
DDC 331.892/8223340975409042—dc23/eng/20240118
LC record available at https://lccn.loc.gov/2024002829

Book design by John Candell
Typeset by Westchester Publishing Services
Printed and bound in the U.S.A.
2 4 6 8 10 9 7 5 3 1

To find out more about our authors and books visit www.bloomsbury.com
and sign up for our newsletters.

*For my father, Clyde Watkins, a mines planning
and reclamation engineer who spent his working
life in phosphate and coal, telling them where
to dig and then how to undo the damage*

TABLE OF CONTENTS

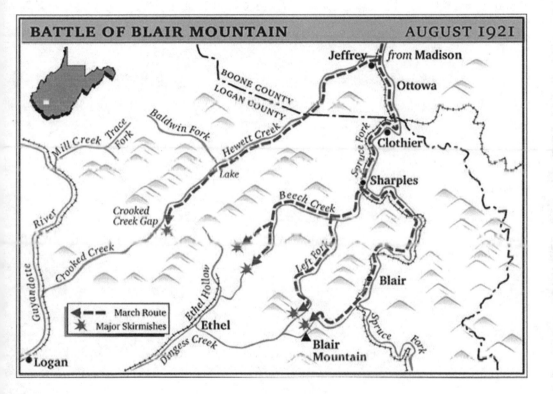

BATTLE OF BLAIR MOUNTAIN — AUGUST 1921

BOONE COUNTY
LOGAN COUNTY

Jeffrey · *from* Madison
Ottowa
Clothier
Sharples
Blair
Blair Mountain

Mill Creek · Trace Fork
Baldwin Fork
Hewett Creek
Lake
Crooked Creek Gap
Crooked Creek
Beech Creek
Spruce Fork
Left Fork
Ethel Hollow
Ethel
Dingess Creek
Spruce Fork
Guyandotte River
Logan

March Route
Major Skirmishes

THE MINE WARS

THE BLOODY FIGHT FOR WORKERS' RIGHTS
IN THE WEST VIRGINIA COALFIELDS

CHAPTER ONE

"One hell of a lot of bloodletting in these hills"

O n May 19, 1920, in the small town of Matewan in the rugged southern coal mountains of Mingo County, West Virginia, a dozen members of the United Mine Workers of America union, most of them out of work, took up hidden positions with their rifles: crouching on rooftops, behind second-story windows, and down side alleys in and around the train station. Waiting. They were there at the urging of Matewan's police chief, tall, lanky, twenty-seven-year-old Sid Hatfield, who locals called "Smiling Sid," or sometimes, because he always carried heavy, "Two-Gun Sid." With Sid Hatfield that day was his friend Cabell Testerman, all five feet five and 170 lbs. of him, the town's mayor, whose other ventures included a local diner and a jewelry store.

Everybody in town seemed to know what was coming. Matewan Grade School had been let out early. Children still out on the streets were hustled out of harm's way and into the basement of the nearby Methodist Church.

It was late afternoon in the dusty town of eight hundred. A few weeks before, the miners had been locked out of their jobs at the Stone Mountain Coal Company, just north of town. And because the Stone Mountain Coal Company also owned most of their houses, dozens had been evicted and were now living on the outskirts of Matewan in union-supplied tents with their families. But they were determined to take a stand, no matter

the consequences. They were sick and tired of the low pay in the mines. The unsafe working conditions. The brutal treatment they suffered under the violent mine guard system. The credit, or scrip, they were paid—instead of cash—that they could only use at the company store.

And they were sick and tired of the ruthless Baldwin-Felts Detective Agency hired by the mine owners to bust up the union and keep the miners in line.

A dozen Baldwin-Felts agents—or, as the miners called them, "gun thugs"—had arrived in Matewan by train earlier that day, on a mission to evict several other mine workers who'd thrown in their lot with the union. The workers were powerless on their own and knew it. Their only hope of forcing change in the mines was by banding together and holding out the threat of a strike to shut down production until the owners agreed to negotiate—not with individual miners, but through collective bargaining with the workers' union on behalf of *all* the miners in southern West Virginia.

The Baldwin-Felts agents' job was to make sure that didn't happen. They had gotten right to work wrecking the workers' homes, tossing their belongings into the street, and daring anybody to get in their way. Some of the mine families stood and stared, helpless to stop

Railroad tracks led right to the heart of the small town of Matewan.

what the Baldwin-Felts men were doing. Some of the miners and their families had gone into hiding, fearful that the agents wouldn't stop at emptying out their houses. Some evicted workers had been savagely beaten at other mines in the past. Some with union sympathies had disappeared or turned up dead.

The famous labor organizer Mother Jones had predicted years before that there would be violence in the southern West Virginia coal mines, and a lot of it. At a union rally at the state capital, she'd told a thousand angry miners they needed to warn the then governor "that unless he gets rid of these [expletive] . . . Baldwin-Felts mine guard thugs there is going to be one hell of a lot of bloodletting in these hills."

The heavily armed agents in Matewan were used to throwing their weight around, protected by a cabal of West Virginia mine owners who considered the agents to be their own private army. The Baldwin-Felts men weren't detectives in the traditional sense. They didn't generally solve crimes. Mostly their job was to serve as armed guards at the mines, strong-arm coal miners who might try to unionize, bust union organizers' heads, and forcibly evict fired workers and their families out of their company homes. Some were spies, infiltrating the ranks of the miners and even living among them in the coal towns.

But on the afternoon of May 19, everything changed— dramatically changed—when the Baldwin-Felts men, after a celebratory meal at a nearby hotel, headed for the depot to board the next train back to company headquarters fifty miles away.

Most of them never made it. Not alive, anyway. Because near the station, blocking the street in front of the hardware store, were Sid Hatfield and Mayor Testerman, both of whom stood solidly on the side of the out-of-work miners. Knowing they had backup—those hidden union men with their guns cocked and ready—Hatfield and Testerman demanded whatever papers the agents claimed to have giving them the authority to kick the miners and their families out of their homes.

Hatfield, who'd grown up working in the mines himself, was one of the few law enforcement officers in West Virginia sympathetic to the miners' union, and he was loud and clear about what was going to happen to the Baldwin-Felts agents if they couldn't prove they had proper authority for the evictions: *he* was going to arrest *them*.

The Baldwin-Felts men, caught off guard, admitted they

"Smiling Sid" used his role as police chief to support the out-of-work miners.

didn't have any official papers. But what they *did* have, the lead detective, Albert Felts, said, was the offer of a monthly stipend—a bribe—to Hatfield if the police chief would look the other way when the detectives came back to town to deal with any more "problem" miners.

Felts had also tried to bribe the mayor earlier, if Testerman would let the agents bring in machine guns and mount them on top of a couple of buildings, just in case things got testy with the union.

Both men turned him down emphatically.

More words were spoken between Felts and Hatfield, calm at first, according to witnesses, the two men even smiling and laughing at one point. But then the conversation got heated. And suddenly, as quick as you can spit, things went sideways.

No one could say for sure which of the men drew first, or which one started the shooting, but in seconds the quiet street turned into a bloody battlefield. The first to go down, mortally wounded, was Mayor Testerman, but it was the Baldwin-Felts agents who got the worst of it from Two-Gun Sid and the hidden miners, some of whom ran into the street to chase down the fleeing detectives.

Over the next twenty minutes, a hundred rounds were fired. Two miners were gunned down. One was fifty-three-year-old Bob Mullins, who'd been fired just that morning for joining the union. The other, Tot Tinsley, who'd been unarmed, was killed by a bullet to his head. The mayor died later that night. His last words, as he was taken by train for help, were, "Why did they shoot me? I can't see why they shot me."

Two Baldwin-Felts agents escaped by swimming across the river into Kentucky—"Split the creek," a woman advised one of them, pointing to the river, when he begged her for help. The other followed suit only after hiding for hours in a trash can. Two more Baldwin-Felts men, though wounded, managed to climb onto the waiting train where they hid until it pulled out of the station.

Seven other Baldwin-Felts men lay dead in the streets, including Albert Felts and his brother Lee. Their bodies were left there for hours until officials from the county seat came over on another train and got them.

The Baldwin-Felts agents killed in Matewan included (clockwise from top left) C. T. Higgins, Albert Felts, Lee Felts, J. W. Ferguson, E. C. Powell, A. J. Booher, and C. B. Cunningham.

When word reached the state capital of Charleston and the United Mine Workers of America office there, one official helping lead the union drive was said to have shaken hands with himself and danced around the room. Another miner there, when he heard the news, said, "Them sons of bitches had it comin'."

But Frank Keeney and Fred Mooney, the president and treasurer of the United Mine Workers, and the two men leading the fight to unionize the southern mines, knew they had a problem on their hands—a *huge* problem—because if there was one thing certain, it was that retribution by the mine owners would be swift and fierce.

The gun battle made national news—in some ways the culmination of two decades of violent clashes between labor and management in mining towns and other workplaces in West Virginia and around the country. In other ways, it was a prelude to what was still to come.

Many soon took to calling it "the Matewan Massacre." The miners, though, protested the name—they preferred "the Battle of Matewan"—saying "Massacre" sounded as though it had been an ambush, and as though they were the ones responsible, when all they were doing was defending themselves. They said it was the Baldwin-Felts agents who deserved most of the blame for getting themselves killed. No matter that several of the agents, after being warned earlier in the day about violating the town's firearm code, had relented and packed away their rifles. Four of them, the Felts brothers included, still had their pistols and still managed to kill the two miners and Testerman.

But besides all that, the miners argued it was actually the coal operators and owners—many of them millionaire investors from out of state—who were at fault, not only for the shoot-out, but also for what preceded it: decades of violence against the miners who toiled day in and day out to put profits into the owners' pockets.

What is indisputable is that the two sides were on a monumental collision course that had been building for years. The miners wanted their union, desperately needed it, so they could bargain collectively for a fair wage, reasonable hours, safety measures, and job protection. After years of stagnant pay during the Great War, when the entire country, and the coal industry most of all, was mobilized for the war effort, the miners wanted what they'd been promised. A monthlong national coal strike in late 1919 had gotten unionized miners a 14 percent wage hike half of what had been promised by President Woodrow Wilson at the end of the war, but at least it was something.

But since the southern West Virginia mines weren't unionized—and the owners swore they never would be—the workers there still toiled day in and day out for the lowest pay in the country, even though their mines produced the most coal and some of the highest profits of anywhere in the world.

The only way to fix things, as far as the workers could see, was to band together to demand change. And after years of repression by the owners' enforcers, those Baldwin-Felts "gun thugs," the miners were ready to take up guns and go to war for what they believed was their inalienable American right to organize.

The mine owners, who saw themselves as noble captains of industry, great defenders of capitalism, had long used violent means to maintain their iron-fisted control over King Coal and the men they paid to extract it from the West Virginia mountains.

They bribed the politicians, they bankrolled law enforcement agencies, and they controlled the courts. There wasn't much they wouldn't do to keep hold of what was theirs.

The Baldwin-Felts agents had made a prosperous living doing the dirty work of these owners, and of course they wanted to keep their jobs. But after Matewan, they wanted something else as well, and a year later they would have it—igniting the greatest armed insurrection in America since the Civil War.

They wanted revenge.

CHAPTER TWO

"Human drift"

Coal mining in 1920 was a deadly business. Nationwide, a thousand miners died underground every year, killed by explosions, cave-ins, and fires. And death had its own language in the mines. "Black damp" was what they called it when trapped workers ran out of oxygen. "White damp" was when miners were caught in lethal pockets of carbon monoxide. "Fire damp" took hundreds of lives when unsafe levels of methane built up and were accidentally, and all too easily, ignited. More than ten times the number who died were injured and maimed in the mines, many of them for life.

The reported body counts from mine accidents were most likely low. Most *definitely* low, as many of the workers who went down into the mines in the late nineteenth and early twentieth century were young boys working off the books, helping their fathers, not officially there, and so, after an explosion or cave-in, not even counted as dead.

In the biggest and worst underground disaster of all time, the twin-mine explosions in Monongah, West Virginia, in December 1907, the official death count was 362. But there were so many boys lost with their fathers, most of their bodies never recovered, that experts, and even the mine manager, said the actual number of deaths was closer to six hundred. The mine operators

After the twin-mine explosions in Monongah, the streets became a makeshift morgue for the dead.

tried to blame the disaster on a boy—not any particular boy, just *some* boy—who they said might have been playing with stolen powder and matches down in the tunnels. The actual cause of the first explosion was the brakes failing on a line of unattended coal cars. The cars careened at high speed down a steep incline from the top of a coal tipple, the structure where rock was loaded onto waiting train cars, back down into the mine. Improper ventilation, the use of highly explosive black powder, a series of secondary explosions, and a lack of backup safety measures were also factors.

With few enforceable safety regulations and no laws in West Virginia requiring companies to compensate the surviving family members of workers who were killed on the job, those left behind depended on charitable donations that in the end came to a paltry $150 for each widow and $75 for every child under sixteen. One of the principal mine owners, the New York multimillionaire John D. Rockefeller Jr., thought that was too generous.

"There seems to be quite as much danger that the public will overdo relief work as that it will not do enough," he wrote at the time, "and I verily believe that quite as much harm is done through the former as through the latter."

Ten days after the Monongah mine disaster, fifty-seven coal miners died in an Alabama mine explosion. Three days later, on December 19, 1907, it happened again, this time in Pennsylvania, where 239 were killed. The grim total that year—officially—was 3,400 deaths.

According to the US Mine Safety and Health Administration, which didn't exist until after the time of the Monongah disaster, the official death toll for coal miners from mine accidents would run to 95,000 nationwide over the first fifty years of the twentieth century.

It was no wonder the mine workers of West Virginia were increasingly willing to fight for the right to form a union. It was the only hope they had.

The coal mine owners, most of them wealthy industrialists, held fast to the hardcore capitalist belief in employment at will, which meant they could hire and fire whoever they wanted whenever they wanted and for whatever reason they wanted. Workers were free to come and go as they pleased as well. At least in theory.

But in West Virginia, where mine owners colluded with one another to keep wages low, costs down, and profit margins as high as they could get them—and employed mine guards to keep their workers in line—the reality was still that a non-union miner could either take the job that was offered or not work at all.

Fred Mooney, who would later become a key leader of United Mine Workers District 17, had learned that lesson the hard way when he was a young husband and father working in the West Virginia coal mines years before all the trouble erupted in Matewan.

"I 'led the sheet,' as was said when one miner did more work than any of the others," he wrote in his autobiography, "but at the end of each month after deductions for house rent, smithing, fuel, doctor, etc., I did not appear to get ahead and of course children were born and had to be cared for."

After three years, the young Mooney threw up his hands

Before Fred Mooney became the treasurer of the District 17 miners union, he struggled to support his family in the West Virginia coal mines.

in despair. "We don't seem to be getting anywhere," he recalled saying to his wife. "Here we are. I have worked and you and I have skimped and tried to save something for a rainy day, and we are right where we started. . . . It is just work, work, and nothing to show for it but a little food, very few clothes, and a hovel over our heads."

When Mooney set out on his day off to search for work at another mine that would pay better, word quickly got around. There were mine guards and spies in the company towns, plus everybody knew everybody and their business no matter how well they might try to hide it. Mooney was promptly fired. And since all the workers' houses were owned by the coal company, who acted as their landlord, Mooney and his family were promptly evicted from their home as well. He became "human drift" as he later called it, until landing another job at another mine that turned out to be no better, no different, than the one he'd left.

From the cradle to the grave, the lives of most coal miners in West Virginia were tightly controlled by the mine owners in

Workers toiled in cramped and dangerous conditions, under the thumb of owners who were far removed from the mines.

these company towns. Workers sent their children to study in company schools. They prayed at company churches and shopped for groceries at company stores, where they also got their mail, first scrutinized by store clerks to make sure no union material was coming in. They paid for everything with company-issued

Most coal companies paid workers in "scrip," a currency that could be used only in company-owned stores and establishments.

scrip—which was only good in the company store, where prices were set at whatever the company wanted to charge.

As one worker explained it at the time, "We work in *his* plant. We live in *his* house. Our children go to *his* school. On Sunday we go to hear *his* preacher. And when we die we are buried in *his* cemetery."

A miner's pay statement lists debt from the company store, doctor and hospital fees, and a burial fund deduction.

One of the more notorious owner-operators was an Englishman and former Methodist minister named Samuel Dixon, who everybody called "King Samuel" because of the imperious way he ruled his coal kingdom. With backing from investors in Boston, Pennsylvania, and elsewhere in New England, he ran a dozen mines in Fayette County, West Virginia. He also published all the newspapers in the region, which kept journalists from writing negative stories about him, and controlled most of the politicians as the Republican Party county boss. When two of his mines blew up in 1906, killing 135 men and boys, a coroner's jury blamed "human error," even though there had been clear violations of numerous safety laws. No one was surprised by the verdict, though, since Dixon had hand-picked the jury, packing it with coal company officials and his political pals. Needless to say, Dixon had no tolerance for the miners' union and little regard for workers' rights or their well-being.

Even supposedly benevolent mine owners, like Edward Stone, from Roanoke, Virginia, strongly opposed the mine workers' union. Stone, a printing magnate and philanthropist who had a controlling interest in the Borderland Coal Company in Mingo County, was known far and wide for his good works—serving on the board of trustees for the Committee to Assist the Blind, supporting Jewish refugees in Russia, donating to the Tuskegee Institute, active in dozens of civic associations. Yet Stone had no reservations about bringing in replacement workers, "scabs," to take over jobs from any of "his" miners who signed on with the union. In one of the crowning ironies of the day, Stone even donated money to a Coal Miner's Relief Fund to help the children of the very miners he'd fired for their union activities.

Dixon lived in West Virginia and Stone in nearby southwest Virginia, both close to the Appalachian region where the bulk of America's coal was being mined. But most of the owners, those wealthy industrialists and their big corporations, lived far away in cities like New York and Philadelphia and Pittsburgh. As

A group of southern West Virginia coal barons gather not long before the mine wars to celebrate a property sale in the New River coalfields.

early as 1810, absentee investors controlled more than 90 percent of what would later become West Virginia, and for years, U.S. Steel, headquartered in New York and Pittsburgh, was the biggest employer in the state. By the late 1910s, the West Virginia mines were producing 90 million tons of coal, with 100,000 men and boys employed as miners. But since there was very little manufacturing in the state, the coal, along with most of the profits from the highly profitable mines, left West Virginia almost entirely. Which meant one of the poorest states in America, though it produced vast wealth for others, stayed dirt poor, with very little opportunity for children growing up except to work in the mines.

CHAPTER THREE

"Judicious mixture"

For mine children in the coal towns of Appalachia, getting an education meant squeezing into a small, uninsulated, one-room schoolhouse—if you were within walking or mule-riding distance. By West Virginia law in 1920, everybody under the age of fifteen was required to attend twenty-four weeks a year, not that everybody did. According to new legislation around the time of the Battle of Matewan, boys could no longer drop out to work in the mines when they were twelve (or even earlier in some cases) the way Fred Mooney, District 17 union president Frank Keeney, and Matewan police chief Sid Hatfield had done—unless a boy's parents signed an affidavit and lied about what year he was born, which many did. If a boy had an affidavit, no matter how young he looked—no matter how young he *was*—most mine operators didn't ask questions.

Girls went to school, too, as long as they still did their chores fetching well water, hand-washing their fathers' and brothers' coal-filthy clothes, tending the coal-dusted garden, raising the goats and chickens, milking the family cow tied up outside eating weeds by the train tracks, cleaning the company-owned shack they lived in, and boiling water to pour in galvanized buckets for the men's "baths" after their ten and a half hours underground in the mines.

"Clean," of course, was just what they called it when everything was swept or dusted or scrubbed with soap. It was impossible to truly banish the black dust, dust that you couldn't help but breathe in your whole life in the mine-pocked hills and polluted valleys of southern West Virginia.

Children who were in school in 1920, or read the newspapers, or listened to the rare radio that managed to catch the even rarer radio signal, knew that the American Expeditionary

A typical school day for children of miners in West Virginia

Force—that is, the US Army, whom everybody called the dough-boys—had gone over to Europe to bail out England and France and in 1918 defeated Germany to end what was called the War to End All Wars. And they did it in no small part thanks to thousands of West Virginia miners, 58,000 West Virginians in all, every one of them supposedly an expert shot, who enlisted and went and fought and either died there or came back in their smart brown uniforms with their Lee-Enfield rifles—in hopes of getting their old jobs back in the coal mines.

A trapper boy stationed at a mine door to control traffic and airflow in the tunnel.

West Virginia children also knew—from word of mouth if not from official statistics—that coal miners in America, and especially nonunion coal miners in southern West Virginia, had a greater chance of being killed in the dangerous mines than the doughboys had of losing their lives on the battlefields of Europe. The death rate in mostly nonunion West Virginia during the war was nearly twice the rate in the fully unionized coalfields of Illinois.

The ever-present threat of injury and death also loomed for the thousands of young workers in the mines, who lied about their ages, or had fake affidavits from their parents claiming they were older, or worked at mines where managers paid them off the books and the owners didn't care. Many quit school— or never attended—to spend brutally long days as "breaker boys," separating out the good coal from throwaway rock once it was mined and hauled to the surface. Even though the job was aboveground, crippling injuries, and beatings if boys didn't work fast enough, were still common. The better money, though much more dangerous, was for these young, unskilled laborers to work as "trap boys" deep underground, standing in the dark, opening and closing doors to channel airflow in the tunnels and control the traffic of mule-drawn coal carts.

"I met one little fellow ten years old in Mt. Carbon, W.V., last year, who was employed as a 'trap boy,'" the progressive reformer John Spargo wrote in his famous 1906 book *The Bitter Cry of Children*. "Think of what it means to be a trap boy at ten years of age. It means to sit alone in a dark mine passage hour after hour, with no human soul near; to see no living creature except the mules as they pass with their loads, or a rat or two seeking to share one's meal; to stand in water or mud that covers the ankles, chilled to the marrow by the cold draughts that rush in when you open the trap door for the mules to pass through;

A 1911 photo of children who worked in a West Virginia coal mine.

to work for fourteen hours—waiting—opening and shutting a door—then waiting again for sixty cents; to reach the surface when all is wrapped in the mantle of night, and to fall to the earth exhausted and have to be carried away in to the nearest 'shack' to be revived before it is possible to walk to the farther shame called 'home.'"

Once they were old enough, really *before* they were old enough, boys like Frank Keeney and Fred Mooney and Sid Hatfield moved on from those jobs to working the coal banks. Day in and day out, miners young and old grabbed pickaxe and dynamite and headlamp and went down into the drift mines where they carved out a warren of rooms to get to the coal seams, leaving pillars of coal standing to hold up the "roof" while they dug.

Once they reached the seams, the colliers—the name for miners who did the actual digging and blasting for coal—laid wooden tracks for their mule-drawn coal carts, then set to work boring deep holes high and low in the seam. They shoved dynamite powder into the holes, crammed in paper fuses called "squibs," then lit the fuses and ran for cover, hoping and praying that the explosion wasn't too big or too fiery. If everything went right, the colliers returned to a pile of loose coal they could shovel into the coal carts for mules to haul to the surface. But if the explosion backfired out of the hole, it could ignite the coal dust or gas in the tunnels and burn or suffocate anybody and anything caught in the way.

"Retreat mining" was what they did once the seams were tapped out—propping the mine ceilings up with heavy lumber while the colliers took down and hauled away the coal in the pillars that had been holding everything up. That was when the threat of tunnel collapse was the greatest.

All the while, mothers and sisters and family members too old or too injured to work in the mines kept the home fires burning and had to live with the knowledge that as dangerous as mine work was, every time the men and boys left the house it might well be the last time.

The main reason for all the company towns, where 90 percent of West Virginia coal miners lived, was because nearly all the mines were located in hidden crevices tucked back in the mountains, away from most towns and cities, in narrow valleys they called "hollows." Matewan, on the Tug River that marks the border between West Virginia and Kentucky, was one of the few independent towns in coal country, but all around it were company-owned camps erected in the remote hollows where coal was plentiful.

The geography gave West Virginia mine owners a notable advantage. Up north, in Pennsylvania and Ohio and such places, the coal was buried deep underground and miners had to take elevators hundreds of feet down into the bowels of the earth to get to it—and then haul it back out the same way. But in West Virginia, the coal could be accessed much easier, in drift mines that opened up right there in the hollows at the base of the mountains. So the miners could mostly make their way to the rich veins of coal by digging horizontally, or at a slight slope, and then sending it back out in mule-drawn carts. Easier access meant cheaper coal, which meant the demand for West Virginia's grew quickly.

The owners, once they found these coal seams and bought up the mineral rights or the land itself, built railroad tracks from the northern cities so trains could haul equipment in and coal out to industrial centers in the Northeast. Prior to World War I, coal was the primary source of heating and energy in America and around the world—and essential to the process of turning iron ore into steel for railroad tracks, buildings, weapons, seemingly everything in a nation rapidly changing itself over from agricultural to industrial.

But tracks to and from the coal were just part of the equation. There was also the not insignificant matter of a place for workers to live, since there were no towns anywhere near the coal mines tucked up in the hollows. Often the owners just put up tents at first, rustic coal camps with no roads, paved or otherwise. Later, they built cheap houses and charged their workers top dollar, taken directly out of their pay, to live there. And of course, as the population grew in these coal camps, it was only natural that the companies build post offices, stores, schools—all of the infrastructure the workers needed. But it didn't take long for the downsides of this monopoly to become apparent as the companies amassed greater and greater power over the miners' lives.

So whatever went on in the mining towns, the owners were in charge, and few outsiders ever got close enough to see. There were few cars and few telephones, and the ones that were

Miners buying goods at a company store, where the only currency accepted was company-issued "scrip."

belonged to supervisors and other mine officials who lived in big houses high up on the hillsides, above the hollows where coal dust turned everything black.

Most everybody else—four out of five mine workers and their families—lived in what were known as Jenny Lind houses: no foundation, no insulation, no electricity, no indoor plumbing. Families, sometimes more than one to a house, shared out- houses and water pumps. Raw sewage ran through ditches next to the streets and emptied into the rivers, leading to constant outbreaks of typhoid fever. Many creeks and rivers, where gar- bage often ended up as well, unless it was burned in open fires or fed to livestock, ran black from the coal dust and runoff that coated just about everything and everyone in the coal towns. Then there were the slower killers: black lung, untreated infec- tions, poverty, and malnutrition. Yet another danger was the deforestation that went along with coal mining, which could bring murderous flash floods, such as the one in 1916 that swept through several Kanawha River Valley mine towns, killing sixty people, mostly miners' wives and children. Most workers had limited access to medical help, and if they were injured on the job, or took sick, and didn't get better right away, they were soon out of work, and their families were soon out of a place to live.

The writer Mary Lee Settle described the Jenny Linds in her memoir *Addie*, about her grandmother growing up in turn- of-the-century West Virginia coal country: "Most of the miners' houses were pathetic. They were built with one board-and-batten layer, and some inner facing between the family and the weather, on stilts with single wood floors instead of basements, with one fireplace for warmth and cooking and heating water for the miner's Saturday night bath. Behind every house a privy had been dug."

To supplement their meager income—significantly less than what union miners were paid in places like Pennsylvania and Ohio, and even nonunion miners in some of the northern counties in West Virginia—many mine families kept chickens and cows. They also grew vegetables in small plots next to the houses. To heat their homes, they either paid a fee for the very coal they themselves had just dug, or sent their children out to steal buckets of discarded coal from what were sometimes called culm banks—giant mounds of impure rock that the children often played on next to the mines.

Still, people came from all over the country, all over the world, for the jobs.

Scots-Irish whites worked the mines to escape the hardscrabble life they had lived before as mountain farmers or because the railroads, in league with the coal barons, had bought the land they had farmed for generations right out from under them.

Italians and Hungarians and other European immigrant miners, many of them out of work in Europe, or displaced by war, arrived by the thousands as the demand for coal outgrew production in the older mines of Pennsylvania, Ohio, and Kentucky.

Most of the Black miners—one out of every four working the coal seams in Appalachia—were former slaves or sharecroppers from the Deep South who migrated to the free state of West Virginia looking for better pay and a better life. Before the Civil War, West Virginia had been part of regular Virginia, but the mountaineers refused to join the Confederacy, and in 1863 they seceded from the Virginia secessionists and stuck with the Union—becoming the thirty-fifth state, with the motto *Montani Semper Liberi*: "Mountaineers Are Always Free."

Pay in the mines depended on how much coal the company checkweighman said a miner had dug that week.

Black miners and their families took West Virginia at its word and were happy to find that they were paid at the same rate as white miners, worked the same jobs, lived in the same shacks, though farthest from the mines in their own segregated area.

A mine owner named Justus Collins came up with the idea of deliberately bringing in the different races and ethnicities to work in the coal mines and live in the mine camps, what he called a "judicious mixture." For Collins, who'd come to West

Virginia from Alabama after the Civil War—where it was said that he got his coal-mining start at the southern tip of the Appalachians running convict labor—managing workers was a matter of divide and conquer. Bring in a good mix of white people, Black people, and foreigners, he preached to the other mine owners, to keep workers divided. They wouldn't trust one another, he said. They'd stick to their own kind. The unions wouldn't be able to gain so much as a toehold.

The owners held fast to strong, and offensive, stereotypes about the different races and ethnicities in trying to figure out what they considered to be the perfect blend.

But Collins's segregated mine camps ended up backfiring on him, ended up backfiring on all the operators in the various owners' associations Collins started in West Virginia. It turned out that what the owners couldn't do was keep the men of different races and ethnicities from getting to know one another at work. Because underground, picking coal, they were all just miners, everybody paid the same rate, everybody working the same jobs. Heck, they could hardly tell one another apart, as dark as it was, and with all their faces—black, white, and foreign—always covered in coal dust.

Which meant eventually they became friends aboveground, too, playing baseball, shopping at the company store, even drinking and carrying on, swapping stories, commiserating about the low pay and lack of safety standards, and the damnable way the company had so much control over every aspect of their lives that sometimes it didn't even seem like they were allowed to be Americans anymore, with those inalienable rights that were supposed to be guaranteed under the Constitution.

For many mine families, young and old alike, the United Mine Workers Union was the heart and soul of the community—where it was allowed.

So it wasn't long before the union talk started. And not long before the United Mine Workers of America, which had been fighting for workers' rights since 1890, realized that the dirt-cheap coal coming out of the nonunion mines of southern West Virginia was undercutting the profitability of union mines everywhere else, and something had to be done about it before owners started looking for ways to de-unionize.

And not long after that, Justus Collins—"Just-US," not "Justice"—brought in the first Baldwin-Felts agents as mine guards and union busters to shut down all that union talk.

CHAPTER FOUR

"You have stood and seen yourselves robbed"

Tom Felts had long earned his reputation as the iron fist of American industrialists. He was a hard man, square-headed with deep jowls and a high sweep of slicked-back hair. He had worked his way up through the ranks of the Baldwin Detective Agency starting in 1895, tracking down escaped fugitives and busting the heads of anybody suspected of stealing from the Norfolk and Western Railroad. The job was more corporate muscle than detective, though he did know how to get information out of reluctant sources. It didn't take long before the founder, William Baldwin, named Felts manager of the Bluefield office responsible for enforcing the coal operators' will on any miners who stepped out of line, from Virginia to Colorado. In 1907, Baldwin made him a full partner. By 1920, Baldwin was sidelined with age, and Tom Felts ran the operation—now called the Baldwin-Felts Detective Agency—the largest private security agency in the country, supplying an army of armed guards, thousands of them, to protect corporate mining interests all across America.

Which meant it was Tom Felts, who'd once been shot in the chest by a fugitive he was chasing and nearly died himself, who had sent his brothers into harm's way in Matewan— forty-six-year-old Lee and forty-two-year-old Albert. Now he was going to have to collect their bodies and bring them home for burial. And after that, he swore to anybody around,

William Baldwin, left, and Thomas Felts in 1912, five years into their partnership.

he would make damn sure Sid Hatfield and the miners' union paid for what they'd done.

His employers in the southern mines, all members of the Williamson Coal Operators Association, just wanted the insurrection, or whatever it was, put down quickly. They were busy recruiting new workers to replace all the miners they were firing in Mingo County for signing union cards, and struggling to keep the mines open in the meantime with skeleton crews. The Matewan Massacre was bad for business.

As soon as he got word of his brothers' deaths, and the deaths of the other Baldwin-Felts agents, an enraged Tom Felts summoned dozens of his men to the agency's Bluefield office on the Virginia–West Virginia border, where they boarded the next train to Matewan, fifty miles away. They were supposed to arrive late that night, but the engineer, afraid of being caught in the middle of another explosion of violence, refused to stop once they got there and so kept running all the way to the next town over, the Mingo County seat of Williamson. It was after midnight when they arrived there, a good six hours since Tom Felts first heard the news. His brothers' bodies, along with the five other Baldwin-Felts victims, were already in Williamson, taken to a funeral home where Felts saw them the next day.

They'd all been stripped of their rings, money, guns, badges, and other valuables. They all had multiple gunshot holes in their clothes and bodies. Some had been shot in the head. Albert had bruises on his wrists and cinders on his clothes, indicating that he'd been dragged through the streets and railroad yard back in Matewan.

As he stood there looking at the bodies, Tom Felts, who kept trophies in his office, including the blood-soaked shirt of a fugitive he'd once shot, was heard to mutter that it clearly hadn't been a fair fight. Otherwise, he said, "our boys would have dropped twice as many as the miners did."

When the District 17 union treasurer Fred Mooney asked Sid Hatfield a few days later why so many of the Baldwin-Felts men had been shot in the head, Hatfield, always practical, told him, "They wore 'coats o' nails'"—meaning coats of mail, or bulletproof vests—"and we were afraid our bullets would not penetrate them."

Tom Felts already had undercover agents in Matewan, posing as union miners and supporters, and he soon sent in others, now not just to control the miners and crush any union activity, but also to investigate the deaths of his brothers and the other Baldwin-Felts men, and to gather enough information and witnesses to convict Sid Hatfield of murder. Most of Felts's "secret service" agents would turn out to be friends and neighbors and coworkers of the men they were spying on, further dividing the community once their identities became known.

The agents all had code names—"Operative No. 9," "Operative No. 31," and "Operative No. 19." Felts got his first lead the day after the Matewan shootout, a letter from one of his spies, rife with spelling errors:

"Dear Tom, Except My sincear sympthey. I am sending you a List of names. The ones checked are Murders & The rest are witnesses. I would advise That They be arrested & Put under bond."

Not long after, another operative, "No. 31," sent a second letter to Felts: "It is generally talked among the men here that Sid Hatfield shot and killed A.C. Felts and [detective] C.B. Cunningham. I have discussed the matter with several eye witnesses, all of whom seem to be of this belief."

Yet another report laid the blame for most of the killings on two men: "Reese [sic] Chambers [owner of the hardware store where the shooting started] and Sid Hatfield received credit for killing the majority of the Baldwin-Felts men."

And just three days after the shootout, an operative reported to Felts the stunning accusation that "the consensus [sic] of opinion among the citizens of Matewan is that Sid Hatfield shot Mayor Testerman himself, for the reason that he is in love with Testerman's wife."

Little by little, secret report after secret report, accounts of what happened in Matewan, at least according to the Baldwin-Felts spies, emerged. And Tom Felts made sure it all ended up in the hands of the Mingo County prosecuting attorney, the grand jury, and circuit court judge James Damron, who would make the final ruling on which men would be indicted for the shootout and on what charges.

All agreed that Albert Felts and Cabell Testerman were the first to go down, but for every witness who said Sid Hatfield fired the first shot, there were two others who claimed it was Albert Felts. There were so many varying accounts that it was impossible to know what was true and what was wild speculation.

One month after the Battle of Matewan, on June 21, 1920, a white-haired, round-faced, eighty-three-year-old Irish woman stood on the steps of the Williamson courthouse in a long black dress and high white-lace dickey. Her name was Mary Harris Jones, but nobody called her that—not in West Virginia, not anywhere in America where working men and women were locked

Mother Jones!

Known in Every Mining Town in the United States as the Great Fighter For Miners' Freedom, will Speak at

MATEWAN, W. VA.
MONDAY NIGHT,
JUNE 21st, AT 7 O'CLOCK

THIS IS A BIG

Mass Meeting!

For All Mine Workers On
TUG RIVER.   ATTEND
And Hear Her Great Message.
U. M. W. OF A. DISTRICT NO. 17.

An exciting speaker would soon arrive in Matewan.

in battle with management. They called her Mother Jones, and on that hot summer day in the Mingo County seat, she was as worked up as ever, glaring down at a large gathering of 1,500 West Virginia miners and giving them hell. They were one sorry bunch, she railed, to have let the mine owners, those "robbers and rascals," walk all over them. She challenged their manhood. Questioned their patriotism. Said it was their own damn fault, the fix they were in, for not standing up for themselves sooner.

It was reverse psychology, and the mine workers, who revered the old lady and had for the past twenty years, loved every word of it.

"You have stood and seen yourselves robbed," she barked at them in her thick Irish brogue. Out of every ton of coal, she said, "so much was taken out, and professional murderers were hired to keep you in subjection, and you paid for it! Damn you, you are not fit to live under the flag. You paid professional murderers

Mary Harris Jones was "Mother Jones" and "the Miners' Angel" to the workers of America and their families.

with that money you were robbed of, and then you never said a word. You stood there like a lot of cowards, robbed by the mine owners. And you let him do it, and then you go about shaking your rotten head—not a thing inside. You call yourselves Americans. Let me tell you, America need not feel proud of you!"

The miners cheered her on and pledged to take up the fight. Those who hadn't yet signed their union cards lined up to do it now, inspired—and browbeaten—by this elderly labor organizer they called the "Miners' Angel," and who called them, lovingly, "My boys." The local clergy and "better" citizens of Williamson, on the other hand, were predictably offended by Mother Jones's speech. All that profanity, they said, was unbecoming of a proper lady. But the miners laughed it off and kept cheering her on, just as they'd done since way back in 1897 when she first set foot in the state she called "Medieval West Virginia" because of the appalling work and living conditions she found there.

Back then, when she'd "only" been in her midsixties, she'd once had to give a union speech while standing in the middle of a stream when mine owners threatened to arrest her for trespassing on their property, which included every square inch of ground for miles in every direction, including the roads. "Medieval West Virginia!" she wrote late in her life. "With its tent colonies on the bleak hills! With its grim men and women! When I get to the other side, I shall tell God Almighty about West Virginia!"

Since losing all four of her children and her husband to yellow fever years before, and then her dressmaking business in the Great Chicago Fire, the Irish immigrant Mary Harris Jones had transformed herself into "Mother Jones," probably the most famous, and unlikely, union organizer in America at the turn of the century and beyond. The workers loved her for her fierce battle spirit and her unmatched success at promoting the union cause. "Get it straight," she once said. "I'm not a humanitarian, I'm a hell-raiser." Industrialists, mine owners, and politicians agreed with the US district attorney who once dubbed her "the most dangerous woman in America."

A week after the June 21 rally, Mother Jones held another in Williamson. By then, the crowd of 1,500 had grown to 5,000 as the union drive accelerated in the aftermath of the Battle of Matewan. Mother Jones gave those 5,000 hell all over again. She'd traveled to Matewan and met with Sid Hatfield and District 17 union leaders Frank Keeney and Fred Mooney, she told them. Those boys were doing their part, she said, standing up for the union, and it was high time the miners of southern West Virginia did theirs.

Keeney and Mooney hadn't just been doing their part since the shootout. They'd also been working nonstop, making their way from Charleston the minute they heard the news to get the lay of the land in Matewan. Though the deaths were tragic—Cabell Testerman, the two miners, even the Baldwin-Felts agents—the union leaders were nonetheless encouraged by what they found: workers in the Mingo County coal mines, fearful in the past of the owners and their mine guards, now appeared emboldened by the stand Sid Hatfield and his "deputies" had taken against the Baldwin-Felts men. Most of the miners had felt—had *been*— beat down all their lives. But now, suddenly, there was something like hope in the air, and Keeney and Mooney were quick to take advantage. They checked in with Mingo County union officials in the cramped, second-floor District 17 headquarters, then went straight to work, traveling up and down the Tug River Valley, recruiting other miners for the union.

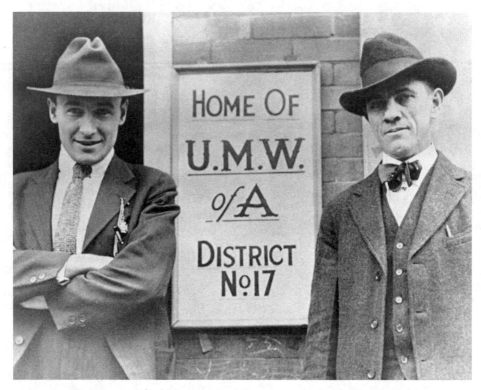

Treasurer Fred Mooney, left, and President Frank Keeney were the driving forces behind the militant United Mine Workers of America District 17.

Within a matter of weeks, with the added inspiration of Mother Jones and her high-octane speechifying, the signed union pledge cards came pouring in. And with numbers finally on their side, Keeney and Mooney were ready to move forward: they approached the mine owners' association to request—to *demand*—negotiations for higher wages and better working conditions and union recognition.

The owners, though, turned them down flat. No meetings. No negotiations. No union miners. Anybody who signed a union card could expect to be fired and evicted from their company houses.

And that was it. With no other options they could see, the union leaders called for a general strike in the Williamson Coal Fields, which included all the mines in Mingo County, beginning July 1, 1920. Matewan, the site of a horrific shootout just weeks before, soon became ground zero for the striking miners, who gathered there on the Fourth of July with their families to celebrate Independence Day with baseball games and barbecue, plus a rousing stump speech by Fred Mooney promising the crowd that a new day was dawning in southern West Virginia.

CHAPTER FIVE

"Bloody Mingo"

Not all the out-of-work miners lived in the union's tent cities. Some moved in with family. Others managed to rent a house or a shack or a room in somebody's home. Some found work to tide them over. One, a man named Charlie Lively, moved to Matewan with his family shortly after the shootout with plans to open a restaurant. Lively had been a friend of Fred Mooney's when they were boys growing up on a small creek near Charleston, though they hadn't seen one another in years. Lively was quick to mention his old connection to the union leader as he made his way around town, while Mooney, always cautious, kept his distance. Lively had returned to West Virginia not long before looking for work and had been briefly hired at one of the nearby mines—and then fired just a few days later for being too friendly with a union supporter.

He found a space for rent downstairs from the District

17 headquarters in Matewan, and in no time at all Lively's restaurant, staffed by his wife and kids, became a hangout for union officials and members, miners and supporters—among them the police chief, Sid Hatfield, who soon became pals with the new owner. A longtime union man with the union card to prove it, Lively talked up the United Mine Workers of America whenever he could. He had worked in mines all over, including out in Colorado where he'd been elected as an officer of the local UMWA during the Colorado Coalfield War of 1914. He'd even done a little jail time there, he said, on account of his union activities.

Lively fit right in with Hatfield and the miners. He was one of them, after all, and it was good to have fellow miners you could count on. Especially one who provided union members with a place to get a hot meal and to air their grievances away from the watchful eyes of mine guards and Baldwin-Felts spies. But what no one could have known at the time was the major role this new guy in town—Charles Everett Lively—would end up playing in the events that followed.

◆

Sid Hatfield might have been an overnight hero to the striking miners, but he was no saint, and everybody knew it. He'd gotten in trouble with the law himself twice in the past year, once for fighting and another time for illegal whiskey. The fight, what the Williamson newspaper called "a good pummeling," had put Sid's foe in the hospital. Sid's version of the events was that the man had been bending over to feed his farm animals, but "one of the pigs grabbed him by the nose and came very near biting it off." Clearly, Sid didn't take the charges against him very seriously.

His friend, Mayor Cabell Testerman, had posted bond for him both times and let him keep his job despite not only these infractions, but also certain unsavory rumors going around about Sid and Testerman's wife, Jessie, that erupted into scandal two weeks after the shootout.

Jessie and Cabell Testerman not long before the Matewan Massacre where Cabell was killed.

It started when one of the Baldwin-Felts spies contacted Felts in early June to let him know that Sid Hatfield had left town and had traveled 120 miles north to Huntington, West Virginia, the state's largest city back then with a population of 75,000 and a number of posh hotels. That in and of itself wouldn't have been a big deal, hardly worth noting, except that Hatfield wasn't alone. With him that day was the newly widowed Jessie Tester-man, and they were checking in together, a room for two, at the Florentine Hotel.

Phone calls and telegrams traveled back and forth between Baldwin-Felts headquarters and their agents and law enforce-ment officials in Huntington. Tom Felts hopped on a train headed for Huntington himself. He wanted to be there when police busted in and arrested Sid Hatfield and Jessie Tester-man for unlawful cohabitation.

The arrest made front-page news in the West Virginia papers, the story inflamed by Tom Felts's accusation at a Huntington press conference: not only did he claim that Hatfield and the late mayor's wife had been having an affair, but he also went on to accuse Sid of murdering his supposed romantic rival and using the shootout as cover. "Hatfield shot Testerman to get him out of the way," Felts told reporters. "The charge that Albert Felts killed Testerman is a dirty vicious lie."

Tom Felts had his story; Sid Hatfield and Jessie Testerman had theirs. When reporters found them at the city jail, Jessie explained that while it was true they weren't yet married, they *had* applied for a marriage license the day before and planned to tie the knot the next day—which they promptly did after paying a $10 fine for their crime of "cohabitation." Jessie said Cabell

Testerman had always considered Hatfield to be a good friend and had told her that if anything should ever happen to him, she should feel free to marry Sid.

Sid had a few things to say about it as well. The allegation that he had anything to do with the death of Cabell Testerman was nonsense. It was Albert Felts who did it. "Felts shot from the hip," he told the newspaper reporters. "He carried two guns. Any other statement is foolish."

Police had found Albert Felts's two guns on Sid's bedside table at the Florentine Hotel and gave them back to a furious Tom Felts.

The Matewan shootout made national news, including a front-page story in the *New York Times*. To many outside West Virginia, though, the massacre—or the battle—had little to do with striking coal miners standing up for themselves. Instead, it was seen as just another example of the violent, backward ways of the Appalachian mountain folk that had defined the region since the old Hatfield and McCoy feud that started shortly after the Civil War. That notorious feud—which involved a different branch of Hatfields than Sid's—had raged back and forth across the Tug River for decades, the two backwoods clans murdering one another in arsons and ambushes until a spate of mass hangings seemed to settle things down once and for all. Though the fighting had ended shortly after the turn of the century, it had generated a conspicuous nickname for the county: "Bloody Mingo."

Now, after the May 19 shootout, people were calling it "Bloody Mingo" for different reasons.

The incident may otherwise have faded from the headlines,

if it weren't for Tom Felts. He pushed sympathetic journalists in West Virginia to run story after story about Sid and Jessie: rumors of their alleged affair, intimations that Jessie had once worked as a prostitute, interviews with unnamed witnesses who swore Sid used the gun battle with the Baldwin-Felts men as a pretext for getting rid of his romantic rival, Cabell Testerman.

The stories never failed to mention that Hatfield, with a long history of violence, had killed a man a few years earlier, a mine foreman, which was true. Sid himself described it as "a little shooting match with a fellow by the name of Wilson" for which he'd been "found clear."

But that didn't stop Felts from labeling Sid "the Terror of the Tug," a name soon picked up by those sympathetic news-papers around the state. "Two-Gun Sid" didn't do himself any favors, either, when he stood in the middle of the street in Matewan and posed for photographers—smiling his gold-tooth smile and holding a pistol in each hand.

Sid played up his nickname by brandishing his signature two guns for newspaper photographers.

When hotel owner Anse Hatfield was murdered in August, shot in the chest one night in Matewan while sitting on his porch, Sid got the blame for that, too. Anse Hatfield—in tight with the Baldwin-Felts detectives and no relation to Sid—had been set to testify as a key witness for the prosecution in the upcoming trial. His family said he'd received a death threat just a few days before he was killed. Witnesses said Sid Hatfield had been sitting on his own porch a few hundred feet away in tiny Matewan at the time of Anse Hatfield's death, but he was charged anyway and so now faced yet another murder count on top of the charges for the deaths of the Baldwin-Felts detectives.

Felts made sure that story got out as well, though the citizens of Mingo County shrugged it off. Two months after the shootout, they elected Sid to be constable for the Matewan district, a step up from his old job as chief of police in the one-cop town.

The union, in a public relations move of their own, had a silent film made and shown throughout southern West Virginia starring Sid Hatfield as himself in a reenactment of the Battle of Matewan—the union's version of it, anyway—along with scenes depicting the harsh conditions for the striking miners in their tent colonies as they continued to hold out against the operators. The movie played in union halls and churches through the rest of 1920 and into 1921—until someone stole the film reel.

The bodies of the seven Baldwin-Felts men, the two miners, and Mayor Cabell Testerman were still warm in their graves, casualties of the Matewan Massacre, but within weeks, the public relations war between the two sides was already in full force.

In many ways, though, the shooting, and Tom Felts's PR attacks on Sid Hatfield, were a sideshow to the very real and painful struggle that had been going on all along in the coal mines and among the miners' families of southern West Virginia. On one side were the fifty-six operators in the lucrative Williamson Field, fighting the union tooth and nail, forcing all their workers to sign so-called yellow-dog contracts pledging to stay nonunion—or else lose their jobs, their company-owned houses, everything.

On the other side was the United Mine Workers District 17 supporting hundreds of mine families—men, women, and children—out of work, living in union-supplied tents, and still emboldened by what they saw as the heroic stand by Sid Hatfield and the miners in Matewan. As far as the miners were concerned, they had only just begun to fight. And it wasn't as if they hadn't taken that fight to the owners before. Their brothers in the Kanawha, West Virginia, mines to the north had, anyway, eight years before—and nearly won. The way the miners saw it, back in 1912–13 during the brutal Paint Creek–Cabin Creek strike, and now again in 1920, they had no choice but to continue the struggle, no matter what.

CHAPTER SIX

"So brothers you can call us"

The United Mine Workers of America had been trying to unionize the West Virginia coalfields for more than twenty years, since even before Mother Jones made her first appearance as an organizer in "Medieval West Virginia" in 1903. That was when she'd first crossed paths with future District 17 UMWA president Frank Keeney, a twenty-one-year-old miner at the time who'd been working underground since dropping out of school at ten to help support his family after the death of his father. Keeney had grown up tough, but resolute. Once as a boy, when a mule crushed him up against a tunnel wall, he bit the mule's ear to make it get off. The mule complied.

As a young man, Keeney liked to take a drink, shoot pool, hunt, all the usual sorts of things when he wasn't working his shift in the mines. He might have lived out his life that way, except that Mother Jones saw something special in him and threw down a challenge.

"I gave him a book one Sunday," she later wrote, "and I said to him . . . 'Go up under the trees and read. Leave the pool room alone. Read and study and find out how to help your fellow miners.' And he did it."

Once he got the reading bug, Keeney never stopped turning the pages, working his way through all of Shakespeare's plays and sonnets, moving on from there to Karl Marx and other Socialist writers who spoke to the very heart and soul of what some called the "workingman's dream": the belief that since laborers knew the technology and the production process in the mines much better than the owners, they were entitled to a greater share of the profits and control.

In April 1912, nine years after first meeting Mother Jones, Frank Keeney, by then an up-and-coming leader of the UMWA, sought her out, hoping she'd come back to West Virginia, this time to help in the Paint Creek and Cabin Creek mines in the Kanawha coalfields. The union had finally made inroads into some parts of the state, including all of the forty-one coal mines on Paint Creek where most of the workers had taken the pledge. They hadn't yet won union recognition from the owners, though, and what was worse, the unionized Paint Creek miners weren't earning any more than workers at the fifty-five *nonunion* mines on nearby Cabin Creek.

They'd tried talking with the operators, Keeney said, had demanded formal negotiations, but hadn't gotten much of anywhere. So the union was calling for a strike in the Kanawha

River Valley coalfields. Maybe if they shut down operations for a
while, the owners would come to see the light.

In June 1912, two months into the strike, Mother Jones
arrived, and it didn't take her long to size up the situation for
herself—and to come up with a nickname for the union-less
Cabin Creek: Russia.

"Here the miners had been peons for years," she later wrote
in her autobiography, "kept in slavery by the guns of the coal
company, and by the system of paying in scrip so that a miner
never had any money should he wish to leave the district. He
was cheated of his wages when his coal was weighed, cheated in
the company store where he was forced to purchase his food,
charged an exorbitant rent for his kennel in which he lived and
bred, docked for school tax and burial tax and physician and
for 'protection,' which meant the gunmen who shot him back

Dirt floors. Raw sewage. Scarce food. Tent life was hard for mine families evicted from their
company homes on Paint Creek during the Paint Creek–Cabin Creek Strike.

into the mines if he rebelled or so much as murmured against his outrageous exploitation. No one was allowed in the Cabin Creek district without explaining his reason for being there to the gunmen who patrolled the roads, all of which belonged to the coal company. The miners finally struck—it was a strike of desperation."

The Paint Creek–Cabin Creek strike of 1912–13 ended up lasting fifteen hard months. By one official count the violence took twenty-five lives—twelve miners, thirteen Baldwin-Felts guards and company men—though other estimates put the number of dead at more than fifty. Dozens more died from malnutrition and exposure and disease, as the mine families, forced out of their company homes and into union-supplied tent cities, huddled together through a long, harsh winter, barely scraping by on their small stipend from the union as they waited out the strike.

By most accounts, the first month of the strike was peaceful. The miners weren't asking for a whole lot. They just wanted the owners to come to the bargaining table. The owners had other ideas, though, and instead of negotiating, they brought in more than three hundred mine guards to reinforce the army of Baldwin-Felts men already in place to police the Paint Creek and Cabin Creek mines. Leading the way were the two Felts brothers, Albert and Lee, who would later be killed in the Battle of Matewan, plus a notorious strikebreaker and army veteran named Tony Gaujot, who'd won the Congressional Medal of Honor while fighting in the Philippines.

When the Felts brothers and Gaujot arrived with the Baldwin-Felts reinforcements, they immediately evicted the mine families who still remained in their Paint Creek and Cabin Creek company houses, forcing more and more women and children and miners into the cramped tent cities. The miners soon fired back, literally, when hidden sharpshooters surprised the agents early one morning with a rifle attack from the forested hills overlooking the mine guards' camp near the town of Mucklow. There were no casualties, but the message was clear: the miners weren't going to roll over this time. The owners could bring in all the Baldwin-Felts gun thugs they wanted, but the miners had plenty of weapons, too, and from now on they were fighting fire with fire, guns with guns.

Tom Felts ordered the guards to fortify the coal mines and sent in machine guns so his men could rake the hills and flush

Armed soldiers were sent in by the West Virginia governor to quell the violence—and control the strikers—during the Paint Creek–Cabin Creek coal mine strike.

out the hidden snipers if it happened again. Armed patrols were sent out to ambush whoever had been doing the shooting. The miners sent out patrols of their own, and the two sides sometimes ran into one another. There were isolated skirmishes all over the mountains. Escalating violence. One man, a miner, was killed. When a rumor got back to the miners that a company of Baldwin-Felts agents was planning an attack on one of the union's tent cities, in Holly Grove, three hundred men grabbed their rifles and stood ready to defend the camp, just in case the rumor proved true. Near the end of July, the miners launched an all-out assault on a Baldwin-Felts encampment nearby that went on for two hours—"a regular hurricane of bullets." At least ten died, men on both sides, in what became known as the Battle of Mucklow.

And the violence didn't stop there. Shortly after Mucklow, miners attacked a train carrying in replacement workers. Dozens of women, working under cover of darkness, tore up railroad tracks so other "scab trains" couldn't get through. The governor of West Virginia, who'd tried his best to ignore what was happening in that rural pocket of the state, finally called in the National Guard, which settled things down—for a while. Surprisingly, it was the miners and their families who were happiest to see the guardsmen, hugging them when a uniformed company of soldiers arrived, shaking their hands, figuring the presence of the National Guard meant at least a temporary halt to the private mine guard system that had prevailed for so many years in the coalfields of West Virginia.

Many in the National Guard were sympathetic to the miners' plight and disgusted with what they saw of the owners' tactics.

Somebody was making a lot of money from coal mining, but it clearly wasn't the workers. "God does not walk in these hills," wrote one of the National Guard officers in his report about conditions in the Kanawha River Valley coalfields. "The devil is here in these hills, and the devil is greed."

National Guard soldiers and local militia show off a cache of weapons at the Sarita Mine in Cabin Creek during the strike.

The mine owners countered by floating a couple of competing conspiracy theories—that unionized mining companies in the Midwest were behind the strike, trying to force their West Virginia competitors out of business, and that Socialists were controlling the UMWA, and their goal was to get rid of the owners altogether and have the workers run, and profit from, sales of the coal they extracted from the mines.

A month later, as soon as the National Guard left, the attacks started up again—on both sides. And as is always the case with armed conflict, it was the noncombatants, the women and children in the union tent camps, who suffered the most. The miners stuck to their guns. The owners brought in reinforcements, even more Baldwin-Felts men to guard their operations, and even more strikebreakers to work the mines.

As fall dragged on into winter, and the suffering and the brutal reprisals continued, the miners formed an underground organization they named the "Dirty Eleven" who took up arms when called upon to run off scabs, shut down mines, defend the tent colonies, and do whatever else was necessary to support the union cause.

The leaders of the Dirty Eleven were a representative cross-section of the different racial and ethnic groups that made up the mining community, Justus Collins's "judicious mixture": the white six-foot-four mountaineer Newt Gump; the much slighter but no less fierce Italian immigrant Rocco Spinelli; and the mighty Dan "Few Clothes" Chain, an African American union man through and through who once got into a brawl almost single-handedly with fifty strikebreakers. Using not much more than his massive size and his fists, Chain convinced the men to climb back on the train that had brought them and head right on back to wherever they'd come from.

A young Fred Mooney, dedicated to the union cause years before he was elected to a leadership position in District 17, was also said to be one of the Dirty Eleven, though in keeping with

Mug shots of striking miners sent to federal penitentiary during the Paint Creek–Cabin Creek Strike. Rocco Spinelli is top row far left, Newt Gump is top row center, and Dan "Few Clothes" Chain is bottom row center.

the secret nature of the group, he said little about it at the time or later in his autobiography.

Whoever else might have been with them, Gump, Spinelli, and Chain worked together, fought together, and even went to prison together on five-year sentences to the federal penitentiary on various counts of assaulting strikebreakers and disrupting the railroads. Dan Chain earned his nickname "Few Clothes" when he got out on early release and returned straightaway to union headquarters still wearing his prison stripes, ready to get back to work, he told the union officials. Whatever they needed him to do.

"So brothers you can call [us] . . . ," a fellow miner wrote at the time in a letter to the union journal, "Negroes, or whites or mixed. I call it a darn solid mass of different colors and tribes blended together, woven, bound, interlocked, tongued and grooved and glued together in one body."

With the violence continuing practically unabated, the governor, William Glasscock, declared martial law on three separate occasions, even going so far as to request federal troops to quash what threatened to turn into open warfare. He used the full powers of the state to shut down the union, doing nothing to address the violent excesses of the owners and their hired guns. The Bill of Rights was suspended. Union and Socialist newspapers around the state were shut down and their editors arrested. The courts were closed, and a military tribunal took over. Hundreds of striking miners and union officials and their Socialist supporters were rounded up, most of them sent to jail, some for lengthy prison terms.

Mother Jones, meanwhile, seemed to be everywhere, urging the miners to stand fast, lambasting the owners. She spent cold nights with mine families in their tent cities, stood in front of a mine guard machine gun at one point and dared them to shoot her, led a hundred mine children on a protest march to the governor's mansion, and was even arrested at a strike rally for reading the Declaration of Independence. In another of her speeches, the ever-defiant Mother Jones held up a bloody jacket taken off a wounded mine guard and declared, "This is the first time I ever saw a [expletive] mine guard's coat decorated to suit me!"

After the second martial law was lifted, in early 1913, union snipers once again fired on the mine guards in Mucklow. The president of the Paint Creek Operators Association happened to be there at the time, and though no one was hit he insisted on retaliation, furious at the thought that he might have been killed. He pressured a local sheriff, one of many in law

Mother Jones firing up the crowd at a gathering of union members and their families in Montgomery, West Virginia, in 1912.

enforcement under the thumb of the owners, and on the night of February 7, he got what he wanted when the sheriff and a dozen gunmen, armed with rifles and a Gatling gun, boarded a double-steel armored train dubbed the Bull Moose Special. As the train rolled past the miners' Holly Grove camp, the gunmen opened fire with their weapons, including the mounted machine gun, shredding the miners' tents and a nearby cabin as sleeping families woke, terrified, and dove for cover. A miner named Cesco Estep was struck in the face and killed while trying to protect his wife and baby.

Estep's wife wasn't able to attend his funeral. She was pregnant and had gone into labor. A weary Mother Jones gave the eulogy. To no one's surprise, the miners soon responded with another attack on another mine guard outpost, killing one, prompting the governor to once again declare martial law—for the third time. And once again, law enforcement and the military came down hard. Hundreds more were arrested—including Mother Jones this time—all of them tried and convicted in military court for murder and conspiracy. The prison sentences ranged from five to twenty years.

When Mother Jones's case was called, she refused to mount a defense. "Whatever I have done in West Virginia I have done it all over the United States," she told the military judges, "and when I get out, I will do it again."

It was all the same to her, she said: "I can raise just as much hell in jail as anywhere." And, she added, in another interview, "If they want to stop my protest against the unjust conditions, the brutal use of force and murder . . . let them stand me against a wall and shoot me."

A new governor, Henry Hatfield (no relation to Sid), had taken office by this time and began working furiously to settle the labor dispute before gunfire erupted yet again. Not even Medieval West Virginia could maintain martial law indefinitely. Though there would be one last spasm of violence in the Paint Creek–Cabin Creek strike—three more men killed—Hatfield eventually succeeded in brokering an agreement of sorts, one the union members were given the choice to either accept or, if they didn't, face being deported from the state.

In the end, the miners made a few modest gains in wages and working conditions. The owners also agreed, on paper anyway, to stop the practice of firing and blacklisting workers who joined the union, and to abide by rulings from a government arbitrations board on future labor disputes.

What the agreement didn't address were the issues of union recognition or the guard system that had brought those hundreds of Baldwin-Felts men into the mines as enforcers and as spies—issues that would be left to fester, barely below the surface, for several more years.

In May 1913, after three months under armed guard and in failing health—and with mounting national pressure on Governor Hatfield—Mother Jones was pardoned and released. Many of the convicted miners were pardoned as well, though not all. Mother Jones eventually recovered and went on that same year to help organize the coal mines out in Colorado, another bloody battle pitting the United Mine Workers union against the mine owners and their Baldwin-Felts guards and spies.

And seven years later, as violence exploded in West Virginia and the union drive caught fire once again, she would be back in the Mountain State, ready to raise more hell.

CHAPTER SEVEN

"The only message you can get out will be to God"

Six years later, a new United Mine Workers of America president, forty-year-old John L. Lewis, decided it was once again time—*past time*—to organize the mines in southern West Virginia. Much of the state had gone union by then, from back before the First World War, after the Paint Creek–Cabin Creek strike. But if the coal mine owners and operators in the southern counties refused to recognize the union and kept getting away with it—keeping wages low and work and living and safety standards even lower—Lewis feared it would undermine everything the UMWA members had fought and died for over the past thirty years. And not just in West Virginia. Coal operators in other states were watching, too, to see what would happen in southern West Virginia. No union there, in the region that had produced a considerable amount of the nation's coal for the war

John L. Lewis led the United Mine Workers of America for more than 40 years.

effort, was a grave threat to the union movement, and collective bargaining, everywhere.

All across the country, in all kinds of industries, unions had been flexing their muscles in the aftermath of the war. In 1919 alone, 4.2 million workers participated in strikes or production slowdowns to force owners to the bargaining table— double the previous high. Corporate owners and stockholders had enjoyed record profits during the war, thanks to lucrative and often noncompetitive defense contracts. Wages for workers, meanwhile, had stayed flat, with union demands shelved and members agreeing to work for less out of a shared sense of patriotic duty. Now, though, with costs high and wages still low, workers nationwide—and the miners in southern West Virginia—believed they were owed.

The first county the union went after, when John L. Lewis announced in 1919 that the UMWA was going to organize the southern West Virginia mines, wasn't Mingo, but rather the one just to the north, which had a notorious anti-union reputation. That was Logan County, which was run—some preferred the word "ruled"—by a man who was more czar than sheriff, though sheriff was his actual title. His name was Don Chafin, and as much as the mine owners hated the UMWA, the union hated Don Chafin even more.

To start off the union drive, the District 17 union leaders—Frank Keeney, Fred Mooney, and the vice president, a fiery younger man named Bill Blizzard—hired and trained fifty organizers and sent them to Logan County to spread out into the coal towns and talk up the UMWA.

They didn't make it very far. Chafin, who in addition to his annual sheriff's salary of $3,500 was also on the payroll of the mine owners' association to the tune of $30,000 a year,

Don Chafin looking dapper in his fiefdom of Logan County, West Virginia.

UMWA District 17 leaders, from left, Bill Blizzard, Fred Mooney, Bill Petry, and Frank Keeney.

had a longstanding practice of ordering his "special constables" to meet every train that entered the county and confront any strangers who got off. If there was even the slightest suspicion that they were union, the deputies gave them a choice: get back on the train and go back to wherever they came from, or spend the night in jail, suffer a severe beating, or worse, and *then* go back to wherever they came from. Sometimes the deputies didn't bother to give strangers a choice in the matter. They just beat them senseless and sent them packing.

That was what happened to the clerk of the State Department of Mines when he showed up for a meeting in Logan and somehow managed to make his way into town. Chafin's deputies, mistaking him for a union organizer, dragged him from his hotel room, spirited him away in a car, and assaulted him so badly that he ended up in the hospital. Others—true union organizers—had also been bludgeoned, or had simply vanished after showing up in Logan and running afoul of Don Chafin's tight rule. The union documented at least nine other cases of men with connections to the union being threatened, savagely beaten, sometimes shot, and run out of Logan.

Later in 1919, when Chafin was tipped off that fifty union organizers were on their way, he dispatched a mob of deputies to wait at the train depot for the union men to arrive. The miners called them Chafin's "Standing Army of Logan," and they outnumbered the union organizers four or five to one.

Threats were made, ultimatums given, and the union organizers, to a man, reboarded the train back to Charleston where they immediately resigned—and that was the end of the attempt to unionize Logan County.

Not that Don Chafin was through with the union. Shortly after, in September 1919 on a visit to the state capital in Charleston, a belligerent Chafin, who had evidently been drinking, barged into union headquarters and confronted the first man he encountered, District 17 vice president Bill Petry. If the UMWA sent any more organizers down to Logan County, Chafin told Petry, he was going to have to take even more drastic measures.

"I'm sorry to hear you say that, Don," Petry responded. "But if that's the way it's going to be, that's the way it's going to be. So why wait? We can shoot, too."

Both men were heeled, as they said back then—carrying pistols. And as soon as Petry spoke, both reached for their guns. Petry got the better of the draw and shot Chafin in the chest.

"He sort of sagged a little at the knees when he was hit," Petry later told Jack Spivak, the labor journalist, "but he straightened himself up and said, 'You going to do a little more shooting, Bill, or may I go to the hospital?"

Chafin survived. Logan County remained impenetrable to the union. And Bill Petry swore he'd throw away his .32-caliber pistol and only use a more deadly .45 from that day on.

After the failed attempt to organize Logan, the union turned its attention to Mingo, the county just to the south, wedged between Logan and the Kentucky line. Actually, Mingo had been a part of Logan County at one time. Dividing Logan into two counties must have made geographical sense back in the day. It was fitting now, at least symbolically, for the different prevailing attitudes toward the union. Clearly, Logan was always going to be hostile, but at least with independent towns like Matewan, the union was able to gain a foothold in Mingo and perhaps build organizing momentum in the southern counties from there.

But it turned out that Don Chafin had a measure of influence in Mingo County, too. After tensions in Mingo County ignited the infamous May 19, 1920, shootout between Sid Hatfield, Mayor Testerman, and the Baldwin-Felts agents, Chafin's teenage niece would become a key witness on the side of the mine owners. She worked as a Matewan telephone operator and claimed she and a coworker had eavesdropped on a conversation between Sid Hatfield and a deputy sheriff in Williamson a few hours before the shooting began. According to the two girls, Sid had called the deputy sheriff to get arrest warrants on the Baldwin-Felts agents for the illegal evictions and had sworn over the phone, "We'll kill those sons of bitches before they get out of Matewan."

This information made its way to Tom Felts, who in turn made sure it would be a centerpiece of the prosecution's case against Sid Hatfield and his codefendants.

Other southern West Virginia law enforcement figures also borrowed from Don Chafin's anti-union playbook. Frank Ingham, one of the many Black union members and organizers for the UMWA, found that out the hard way in the summer of 1920 in the aftermath of the Matewan shootout. After having mined coal in Mingo County for fourteen years, earning an average of $4.50 a day, Ingham was one of those summarily fired and then blackballed for joining the union. His wife was able to hold on to her job as a teacher at one of the all-Black schools, but Ingham bounced around working odd jobs in the mine towns of Mingo and elsewhere. He also stayed active in the union, delivering coal to the tent colonies and building platforms so mine families wouldn't have to camp out on dirt floors. Like many African American miners, Ingham felt at home in the UMWA, which was one of the few unions that had declared it wouldn't discriminate based on race or ethnicity. They'd even written it into their constitution: "No local union or assembly is justified in discriminating against any person in securing or retaining work because of their African descent."

On August 10, 1920, a month after the strike call in the Williamson Coal Fields, Ingham was arrested in Williamson by a Prohibition officer, though he wasn't charged with anything. He'd been on his way to visit his sister. When Ingham protested, the officer threatened to kill him. "Shut up," Ingham said he was told. "Don't open your mouth. I will blow your brains out."

Instead of being let go, no charges of any kind having been brought against him, Ingham was transferred to McDowell County, the next county over from Mingo, where he was thrown in jail by the sheriff, S. A. Daniels. Ingham asked if he could call his wife back in Mingo County, who must be worried wondering what had happened to him, but Daniels denied the request. "The only message you can get out will be to God, and unless you hurry you will fail in that," Ingham was told.

Ingham was left in a cell for several hours, certain he was going to be killed. His suspicions were confirmed at midnight when the sheriff showed back up at the jail, unlocked Ingham's cell, and forced him outside where two cars were waiting in the dead of night. "I want to carry you down the road," Sheriff

Daniels told Ingham. "There is some men down there that want to talk to you."

When Ingham didn't immediately comply, one of Daniels's men struck him over the head with an iron club, then tied him up and threw him in one of the cars. Somewhere outside the town of Welch, Daniels's men dragged Ingham into the woods where he was kicked over and over and beat with more iron clubs. They took what money he had in his pockets, a train ticket, even an IOU from a man who'd loaned Ingham some money, and left him there for dead.

Ingham waited until the men and automobiles were gone and he could no longer hear their engines, then dragged himself away to find help. He managed to beg a ride back to Mingo County and his wife, and eventually was able to continue his work for the union and the striking miners, doubling down on his commitment to the miners' cause against the brutality and unfairness they faced—not only from the mine owners, but also from the sheriffs and other law enforcement officials like S. A. Daniels and Don Chafin who abused their positions to protect the owners' interests.

CHAPTER EIGHT

"If thou dost not sow, thou shalt not reap"

After the strike call in the Williamson Coal Fields in the summer of 1920, and once the Mingo County mine owners finished evicting the union miners and their families, 10,000 southern West Virginians suddenly found themselves homeless, thrown out of their company houses, their belongings tossed on the streets by the Baldwin-Felts agents and mine guards. Some moved in with other family members or were able to scrimp together enough money to rent private shacks. Most, though, had nowhere to go.

The United Mine Workers of America had already brought in hundreds of tents for locked-out workers, just as they had done during the Paint Creek–Cabin Creek strike, and now as the strike wore on and more and more union families found themselves homeless, they brought in hundreds more. They rented land for the tent colonies as close as they could get to the mines, not just in Matewan, but throughout Mingo County as well. The miners and their families bought what food they could afford with a meager stipend drawn from the strike fund that UMWA workers from all over the state had paid into with their union dues, plus whatever donations were forthcoming from union sympathizers.

Fired workers line up outside the hardware store in Matewan, West Virginia, on Union Relief Day.

The mine owners, meanwhile, started recruiting new workers far and wide throughout the South and even over in Europe, paying for ship berths, train tickets, and bonuses but often failing to mention the situation in the southern West Virginia counties. That situation, also a replay of the strike from eight years before, involved the union men, and many of their wives, greeting the trains bringing in the strikebreakers and convincing them to get right back on those trains and make it a round trip back to wherever they came from. Or else.

The "or else" quickly got out of hand. Union sharpshooters took up hidden positions in the hillsides overlooking the mines and took potshots at any strikebreakers who dared to make the trip from boarding houses and company-owned shacks to the drift mouths and into the mines.

Mother Jones, of course, had a thing or two to say about the strikebreakers. "I know how a scab is made up," she'd once told the delegates at a UMWA convention. "One time there was an old barrel up near heaven, and all of heaven got permeated with the odor. God Almighty said, 'What is that stuff that smells so?' He was told it was some rotten chemical down there in a barrel and was asked what could be done with it. He said, 'Spill it on a lot of bad clay and maybe you can turn out a scab.'"

The West Virginia governor sent in state police, but they failed to tamp down the violence.

Shortly after the strike was called, a grand jury brought twenty-three murder indictments against Sid Hatfield and the miners who'd backed him up in the May 19 gun battle with the Baldwin-Felts men. The first trial, for the killing of Albert Felts, was scheduled for January 1921. Thanks to Tom Felts and his operatives—bought and paid for by the coal operators of West Virginia and their corporate owners—the prosecution would have plenty of evidence and numerous witnesses, more than enough, they were certain, to put a rope around Sid Hatfield's neck, or at the very least to put him and his mates behind bars and keep them there for years to come, and take all the air out of the strike while they were at it.

As summer 1920 dragged into fall, what had at first seemed promising for the union in the wake of the Matewan shootout started to go south.

Try as they might, with verbal and even physical intimidation of the newly arriving strikebreakers, the out-of-work miners couldn't turn away enough of them to keep the mines from operating. The union snipers hiding near the mines to scare away the scabs were soon run off themselves by Baldwin-Felts detectives and state police. Federal troops were called in twice. A US district court even went so far as to issue an injunction making it illegal for the union to have any contact whatsoever with the strikebreakers, or even mention to any of them that there was a strike going on.

And back and forth it went. Shots were exchanged. Arrests were made. Miners' guns were confiscated. Baldwin-Felts spies named names and tipped off state police to the miners' guerilla actions. There were raids on the tent colonies, though nothing as bad, at least not so far, as what happened during the Paint Creek–Cabin Creek strike with the Bull Moose Special.

A number of the striking Mingo County miners caved, beaten down by cold, hunger, frustration, and despair. They disavowed their union memberships and went back to their old jobs in the mines—if the often-vengeful owners would have them.

And within a few months, with them and the thousands of imported strikebreakers back working the coal seams, most of the southern mines were operating at or near capacity. The West Virginia owners' profits for 1920 totaled $198 million— the equivalent of $2.3 billion today.

A union barracks during the 1920 coal strike in West Virginia, defiant in the dead of winter.

But many more of the striking miners—and their families— held firm, enduring the harsh conditions in the tent colonies that dotted the landscape throughout Mingo County. Just how harsh those conditions came to be, as fall gave way to winter in the stone-cold hollows and mountains of West Virginia, was described by a visiting journalist in *The Nation* magazine:

"Huddled under canvas that flapped and strained at the guy ropes, in the high winds, I found hundreds of families gathered about pitifully small fires. In most cases, the tent dwellers were living on the bare frozen earth, the most fortunate having simply a strip of oil cloth or carpet as floor. Several children have died of pneumonia and it is pitiful to see any number of new-born babies there—and worst, many pregnant women."

Another reporter wrote about following a barefoot child through a camp outside Matewan to the tent where the child had been living. "Inside, on a 'cot' improvised of bricks and sand, a woman was writhing in pain. By her side sat a skeleton-like man, coughing desperately. On the bare frozen ground these barefoot children sat huddled together holding hands over a miserable little wood fire. The tent sagged and strained under the whipping of the wind."

At Christmas, Mother Jones showed up at the camps with wagonloads of presents and clothes for the children who'd been living in those dirt-floor tents since July, just as she'd done eight years earlier during the Paint Creek–Cabin Creek strike. But there didn't seem to be much sympathy for the strikers otherwise. Both the Red Cross and the local chapter of the YMCA refused to offer the tent families aid of any kind. The strike and the plight of the miners, they said, was "no act of God."

And to make matters worse, as if that was possible for the families suffering in their union tents through the bitter West Virginia winter, the striking miners were increasingly seen by many West Virginians and by people across the country as being somehow un-American for standing up for their right to bargain collectively.

Because wasn't that how things had gotten started with the Bolsheviks in Russia? Hadn't the workers, the Bolsheviks—the *Communists*!—taken over all businesses and industry there? The American Way was supposed to be all about capitalism. In his famous essay "The Gospel of Wealth," which he'd published

Striking miners show their loyalty to the union cause—and to America.

about thirty years earlier, the industrialist Andrew Carnegie
had touted the virtues not only of capitalism, but also of wealth
concentrated in the hands, and under the control, of the exalted
few. Men like, well, Andrew Carnegie. Competition, he preached,
was the very heart and soul of a great society, and everybody—not
just the wealthy—benefitted from it, far more than they would
in a Bolshevik-run society. "The Socialist or Anarchist who seeks
to overturn present conditions is to be regarded as attacking the
foundation upon which civilization rests," he wrote, "for civilization took its start from the day that the capable, industrious
workman said to his incompetent and lazy fellow, 'If thou dost
not sow, thou shalt not reap,' and thus ended primitive Communism by separating the drones from the bees."

The coal mine owners of West Virginia couldn't have agreed more. And to their way of thinking, these labor unions weren't just out for more money or improved working and living conditions, but they were also out to destroy the very foundation of capitalist America.

The so-called Red Scare—a fear that socialism and communism might spread from Russia to other countries, might gain a foothold in the United States—had already led to mass arrests and deportations, even lynching and executions, of those suspected of plotting against the American Way. Under the Sedition and Treason Acts passed during the war—and still in effect in the postwar years—even speaking out against the United States sending troops to Europe might be illegal. The Bolsheviks, after they took over the government in Russia, had pulled out of the fight against the Germans. It only stood to reason that anybody who opposed the war must be a Bolshevik sympathizer, too. The American Socialist Party leader Eugene Debs, who received nearly a million votes when he ran for president in 1912—6 percent of the total—was given a ten-year prison sentence for his speeches opposing US involvement in the war.

And the way a majority of Americans saw it—and believed, since they read it over and over in newspapers and magazines— the socialists were clearly in league with the labor movement, so they must all be a bunch of Reds, out to destroy America: from the imprisoned presidential candidate Debs all the way down to those hardscrabble West Virginia mine families huddled in their winter tents next to the coal-train tracks, trying to find a way to survive until spring.

That was how Baldwin-Felts owner Tom Felts saw it, too.

"The miners and their families living throughout the Western fields were living in peace and happiness and enjoying as great prosperity as any coal field in the United States," he told a reporter ten days after the Matewan Massacre. "And it was the Bolshevistic teaching of these emissaries which resulted in our men being wantonly and maliciously murdered through one of the foulest plots that ever disgraced a State."

CHAPTER NINE

"I reckon you thought I had horns"

January 1921 started off with a bang in Mingo County. Literally and tragically. At seven in the morning on Monday, January 12, ten cases of mining explosives detonated in one of the Superior-Thacker Coal Company's storage buildings. Nobody ever found how or why. The giant blast shook every building for a mile around in the county seat of Williamson, breaking glass windows in every storefront and home and showering the town with fragments of what was left of the body of a mine foreman. If the explosion had happened ten minutes later, dozens of miners, lining up to get their allotment of dynamite for the day's work in the mine, would have been killed as well.

On the one hand, it was just another in a long line of industrial mishaps that continued to take the lives of mine workers and inflict massive damage on the surrounding area.

On the other hand, with Sid Hatfield's trial coming up just

two weeks later—to be held in the now nearly windowless Williamson it might have been seen as an omen, a warning even, of the political powder keg in southern West Virginia that was also threatening to explode.

Things blew up even before the trial started. First, it was ruled that the four Baldwin-Felts agents charged with killing the mayor and the three miners would be tried not in Mingo, but up north in friendlier Greenbrier County, where they were all but certain to be acquitted—which is in fact what ended up happening.

Much more disturbing, at least to Sid Hatfield and his twenty-two codefendants, was the announcement that Mingo County Circuit Court judge James Damron, who'd overseen their indictments on those multiple murder charges of the

Defendants in the Matewan Massacre Trials. Sid Hatfield is back row center. His friend Ed Chambers is back row third from the right.

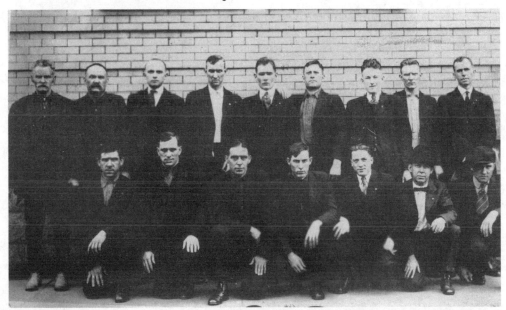

Baldwin-Felts men, had resigned from the bench and joined the prosecution team, which also included a retired state supreme court justice and the longtime attorney for the Williamson Coal Operators Association—all bought and paid for by the mine owners' association. And if money got a little tight for the prosecution, Tom Felts himself, still hell-bent on revenge for the deaths of his brothers, offered to throw in some cash, too.

The union, meanwhile, already stretched thin supporting the striking miners, would have to foot the bill for all twenty-three defendants.

Word got out about who was paying for what, but nobody raised a stink. The miners were used to having the deck stacked against them.

It seemed to take forever to pick a jury. They were shipped in by the trainload—men in overalls, mostly, farmers and miners from throughout the county, a thousand when all was said and done, and four hundred of them interviewed to get it down to the required final number of twelve.

Sid and his codefendants, their bond revoked during the two-month trial, sat in a small jail behind the Williamson courthouse biding their time, though they eventually got a little more leg room when charges were dismissed against five of them and their number dropped to eighteen. Friends and neighbors and supporters plied them with more food and drink than they knew what to do with. In court, Sid wore a brand-new spiffy brown suit he'd bought just for the occasion, while Jessie, his new wife

Sid and Jessie Hatfield, married.

and widow of the murdered Cabell Testerman, wore a string of pearls.

Was he worried? a reporter asked Sid as the proceedings began.

Nah, he answered. "It means no more to me than taking a chaw of tobacco."

On the first day of the trial, somebody noticed a couple of tell-tale bulges under Sid's coat and reported to the judge that Two-Gun Sid had come into the courthouse heeled. When the nervous judge announced that there would be no weapons allowed in the court, a smiling Sid gave up his pistols. Hoping to counter the various character assassinations of him being pushed by the Baldwin-Felts agents, he also made himself available for interviews with the dozen newspaper reporters from all around the country who'd come to cover the trial.

"I reckon you thought I had horns," he said to one. "It's the limit what I read about myself."

Even before the trial began, he was happy to offer up his side of the story, which he described as "just a little free-for-all."

"It was a question of life or death for me," he told a reporter with the *Philadelphia Public Ledger*. "I did no more than other men would do. I was backed against the wall. The detectives surrounded me. . . . Mayor Testerman was in the rear. The detectives had a warrant for my arrest. Testerman said it was bogus. Felts drew his gun and shot Testerman, then swung his gun over his shoulder and shot Brewer [a friend of Sid's who was shot in the chest but survived]. I drew two guns. One was shot out of my hand. A second later a bullet tore through my hat. I started firing as rapidly as I could. It was all over within two minutes."

A variety of witnesses for the prosecution told a different story. Or, rather, a different set of stories, as few of their details seemed to line up with one another, and many fell apart under cross-examination or when contradicted by defense witnesses.

A mine guard, Joe Jacks, swore he'd heard Sid just before the shooting started threatening to "go out and kill the last damned one of them." He said Sid had sent him word that if Jacks testified to this, "I would be did the way Anse Hatfield went."

Matewan hotel owner Anse Hatfield, no relation to Sid, had planned to testify against Sid until he was gunned down a few months before the trial. Sid was charged with the murder, though he never stood trial for it. Witnesses said he'd been sitting on his porch when Anse Hatfield was shot. But people like Jacks still had their suspicions.

But the defense attorneys had their own witness who contradicted Jacks's account. The woman who had supposedly delivered the threat from Sid said under oath that not only had she never given Jacks such a message, but she didn't even know Sid Hatfield. After her testimony, the woman, Stella Scales, went over to Sid at the defense table and introduced herself while everyone in the courtroom looked on. A polite Sid shook her hand and turned and introduced Stella to his new wife, Jessie.

Harder for the defense to undermine was the testimony of the two teenage telephone operators, one of them Logan County sheriff Don Chafin's niece, who said they'd overheard Sid on the phone telling a Mingo County deputy sheriff in Williamson, "We'll kill those sons of bitches before they get out of Matewan." Hard to undermine, that is, until the defense put the deputy sheriff, Toney Webb, on the stand.

Did Sid, in fact, say any such thing? Webb was asked.

"No sir," he responded. "I never heard Sid Hatfield make such a statement in my life, whether over the telephone or otherwise."

And so it went. One of the defendants, Isaac Brewer, Sid's friend who'd been badly wounded in the shootout, surprised everyone by turning on his fellow miners. He testified that Sid had started the massacre when he muttered, "Let's kill every damn one of them," and then shot Albert Felts. According to Brewer, Felts didn't quit breathing right away, not until another defendant, William Bowman, finished off the job, standing over Felts, aiming his pistol, and saying, "Now I guess you'll die."

But then it came out that Brewer, in addition to having the

charges against him dropped in exchange for his testimony, had been paid $1,000 by the prosecution as a "reward."

The biggest surprise among the prosecution witnesses was yet to come, and his appearance when he showed up in the courtroom couldn't have caused a bigger stir. It was Charlie Lively, the union man turned restauranteur, Sid Hatfield's pal and confidante, and, as it turned out, a Baldwin-Felts spy, known on his secret reports to Tom Felts as Operative No. 9.

The defendants, their families, the defense attorneys, everyone in the courtroom and back in Matewan were shocked stone-cold when Lively took the stand and revealed for the first time that not only was he no friend to the miners, and no true friend to Sid, but he'd also been collecting information on them in his restaurant downstairs from union headquarters all this time.

Lively hadn't fabricated his entire backstory: he had in fact worked as a miner and had in fact been a long-standing member of the UMWA. "A slight man of medium height," was how the labor journalist Jack Spivak described him, "with skin drawn tight over his cheekbones, a soft, almost apologetic voice and cold eyes." He'd been born and raised in a company mining town on Paint Creek where he'd been friends with Fred Mooney when they were boys, just as he'd said, and just as Mooney had confirmed, though Mooney later said he'd never actually trusted the guy.

"Lively and I were born and reared in the same community and at one time belonged to the same local of the United Mine Workers of America," Mooney wrote years later. "However, somewhere in my subconscious mind there lurked a suspicion that all was not right with Lively."

When Lively invited Mooney one evening to come home with him for dinner, Mooney, concerned about the possibility that it was a setup, declined. When it came out a year later at Sid Hatfield's trial that Lively was a Baldwin-Felts spy, Mooney was glad he'd followed his instincts to steer clear of the guy. He just wished he'd known enough to warn the others in Matewan.

Every miner and union official in Matewan would have been wise to be suspicious of Lively, but the strikers, happy for any allies, had welcomed him into their town and their lives. He was one of them, after all—or so he kept reminding them, as he denounced the mine guard system, promoted the union, and even assisted in planning and carrying out acts of violence in support of the striking miners. For him to turn around and blame the strikers for this very same violence, as he testified against them in court, was an unimaginable betrayal against the brotherhood the miners so fiercely defended.

"C. E. seemed to think duplicity was an honorable trait," one of Lively's sons wrote in a letter years later. "He would sign men up for the union and then turn these mens [sic] names over to the Felts Detective Agency. . . . He usually referred to the union men as Reds. And any of them were killed was one less Red to deal with.

"I know up until I was 12 I was terrified of my Father, He had a split personality and was a different person from one day to the next."

Charlie Lively had been working undercover on the Baldwin-Felts payroll for years, deceiving his fellow miners so well that they once elected him as a delegate to the UMWA convention. Several years earlier, when labor conflicts had died down for a while in West Virginia, he'd been sent by Baldwin-Felts to spy on coal miners who'd gone on strike out in Colorado. Albert Felts had been sent out to Colorado, too, and put in charge by his older brother Tom of operations against the miners trying to unionize there. Felts paid Lively, working undercover there as well, to get himself arrested and serve time in jail with other strikers so he could collect information about their plans from the inside. Lively went on to kill another man in a prison fight, though he was never charged. He got out after eighteen months, got paid by Baldwin-Felts, and went home to West Virginia for his next assignment—in Matewan.

CHAPTER TEN

"If there's an agitator around you can just stick him in jail"

Despite all the promises of explosive insider revelations, Charlie Lively's star testimony for the prosecution turned out to be a bust, hardly worth the clandestine life he and his family had led—on the Baldwin-Felts payroll—for much of the past year. Lively's wife and children had already left Matewan, abandoning their home and the restaurant, as he sat in the Williamson courtroom and repeated all the various confessions he'd supposedly heard from Sid Hatfield and four of the other defendants about the shooting of Albert Felts and the other agency men. It was a detailed story of defenseless Baldwin-Felts detectives running for their lives, being chased down and executed, one after another, by a murderous Hatfield and a heartless gang of miners.

Among Lively's claims:

Sid told the Baldwin-Felts spy, his supposed friend, that he'd shot Albert Felts but hadn't killed him.

A miner named Art Williams bragged that he had finished off a fallen Albert Felts with a shot to the head.

Reece Chambers, the hardware store owner, told Lively he'd shot and wounded Albert's brother Lee.

Another miner, Fred Burghoff, said he'd been the one who killed J. W. Ferguson, a former police chief who'd gone to work with the Baldwin-Felts Detective Agency.

And not only had the detectives been killed in cold blood, and not only had Sid started the whole thing off by shooting Albert Felts, but Lively also repeated the pervasive story that Sid had killed the mayor, Cabell Testerman, because Sid had long coveted Testerman's wife, Jessie. Tom Felts had been making sure for the past several months that the allegation was mentioned in sympathetic newspapers willing to publish the salacious rumors, but now here it was, coming from Charlie Lively, in the biggest murder trial in West Virginia history:

"Did Sid Hatfield make any statement to you at any time as to who killed Testerman?" Lively was asked in court.

"Yes, sir he did."

"Who did he say killed Mayor Testerman?"

"He said he did."

"State to the jury in what way he made that statement."

"We were talking about the killing. He said after Albert Felts was shot he shot Mayor Testerman. Testerman was getting too well lined up with those Baldwin men."

But Lively's testimony, too, fell apart under cross-examination, especially when it came out that he had been on the Baldwin-

Felts payroll for the past ten years, was banking a cool $225 a month, plus expenses, and hadn't been anywhere near Matewan the day of the shooting. Not only that, but Lively was also forced to admit that he'd been complicit in arming the miners, even going as far as illegally buying a machine gun on orders from Tom Felts and bringing it back to Matewan.

As for all the conversations Lively supposedly had with the various defendants—including Sid Hatfield? All were denounced as hearsay, and all were denied by the men who Lively, through lies and deceit for much of the past year, had convinced were his friends.

The defense attorneys hammered away at Lively's duplicity, at the attempted bribery of Sid Hatfield, and at the successful bribing of Isaac Brewer that turned him against his fellow defendants. They talked about the ways the coal mine companies—all those big corporations and absentee owners—had for years hired heavily armed Baldwin-Felts gun thugs to brutalize and control the Mingo County mine workers and their families. They praised Sid Hatfield and his fellow defendants for being willing to stand up to the Baldwin-Felts detectives.

In the end, after forty-six days of back-and-forth testimony, the Mingo County jury wasn't buying a lick of what the prosecutors were trying to sell. And as for Charlie Lively, well, he was nothing but a sorry traitor to the cause, his union membership immediately revoked after his testimony. Not that there'd ever been much chance of a conviction anyway.

"They still tell how the jury reached its verdict," wrote journalist Lon Savage. "One of the jurors, a farmer from the little town of Gilbert far back in the mountain wilderness, had looked at the other jurymen and then looked out the window at the mountain. When the trial started, he said, the mountains were brown and bare. Now the trial was ending, and the mountains were turning green and the dogwood and laurel were about to bloom. He was ready to sit there, he said, until the mountain turned brown again and the dogwoods bloomed again before he'd vote to convict a single Matewan boy."

The trial was over. The verdicts, not guilty. A crowd of hundreds was waiting at the train station when Sid and the miners returned to Matewan, acquitted in the shooting death of Albert Felts and out again on bond for the deaths of the other six detectives. The wild celebration lasted well into the night.

"It's the happiest day Matewan ever knew," someone was overheard telling Sid.

"At least for me," he responded. "It's good to know you have so many friends."

There would be other trials down the road, but the prosecution would never get convictions on any of the Matewan boys. Sid Hatfield faced charges for the other Baldwin-Felts killings, too. But when they called the docket in those subsequent trials, he wouldn't be there to answer.

Charlie Lively might have left town in a hurry, but Sid Hatfield hadn't seen the last of the man he'd once called his friend.

There had been sporadic violence all during the fall of 1920 in the buildup to the trial. The striking miners, kneecapped by the yellow-dog contracts, faced imported strikebreakers; Baldwin-Felts gun thugs; armed mine guards; state police;

federal troops; court injunctions barring them from trying to persuade nonunion workers in any manner, shape, or form to join their cause; and the threat—and soon enough the reality—of martial law.

They fought back the only ways they knew how, or, as they saw it, with the only means they had left: with their fists, their dynamite, and their guns. That October, hidden gunmen— everybody assumed they were striking miners, though nobody ever took credit—shot up a truckload of nonunion workers and wounded two. Shootouts at two other mines soon followed. A man was killed.

In November, the violence escalated, with more men on both sides shot, and some killed, in open gun battles. A coal tipple at

Members of a "Flying Squad" of the anti-union Mingo Militia pose with their car and guns.

one mine—for loading rock onto waiting train cars—was dynamited. Somebody blew up a railroad trestle near another mine. Buildings were set on fire, including a company store near Matewan. Striking miners shot up a passenger train carrying scabs. One of the miners was killed in return fire.

The West Virginia governor sent in soldiers once again to patrol the streets of Matewan and other Mingo towns. Public assemblies were outlawed.

Things were dicey all through the winter and stayed that way through January 1921 during the trial. Shortly after the judge gaveled the proceedings to order, and revoked the bail on Sid Hatfield and his codefendants, union members got word that Williamson was crawling with armed Baldwin-Felts detectives. Worried about the safety of Sid and the other prisoners, a thousand out-of-work miners grabbed their guns and threatened a mass march on the courthouse. Tom Felts, under pressure from the judge, agreed to send his detectives back to Bluefield and the crisis was averted.

As the trial had progressed, reports came in about still more sniper assaults on reopened mines. The whole county was on edge. When a car backfired outside the courthouse, everyone scattered, thinking the shooting had started up there as well.

In February, in Fayette County next door to Bloody Mingo, a running gun battle between union men and mine guards left an entire town burned, dynamited, and so shot-through with bullet holes as to be uninhabitable. It was reported that there might still be some dogs wandering around, but all the residents, fearing for their lives, had left.

If there was a truce in the aftermath of the not-guilty verdicts, it didn't last long. All through the spring, snipers hidden on the Kentucky side of the Tug River blasted away at West Virginia mines across the water, taking aim at the mine guards and scabs who'd stepped into union members' jobs. The Kentucky National Guard was called in, but not before somebody blew up a coal company power plant.

But that was all just a prelude to what came next. Looking back on it later, they called it the Three Days' Battle. But all anyone knew at the time was that when dawn broke on Thursday, May 12, 1921, all hell broke loose in West Virginia.

For a few days, those snipers on the Kentucky side of the Tug had been targeting the town of Merrimack, not far from Matewan, but on May 12 they upped the ante into a full-on assault there on the strikebreakers' camps at the White Star mine. The scabs and mine guards, armed to the teeth, returned fire in a battle that raged back and forth all day and into the night. Strikers cut telephone and telegraph lines, riddled the mine buildings with bullet holes, and waged attacks not just in Merrimack but wherever they suspected scabs were hiding out in Matewan, too. People hid in closets, afraid for their lives if they ventured out onto the streets in either town. Even the state police headquarters in Matewan got lit up in the crossfire. Observers estimated 10,000 shots were fired in all.

One of those bullets killed a prohibition officer named Harry Staton, who was walking near the railroad tracks in Matewan not far from where he lived. That particular shooting turned out not to have been random; Staton had testified against Sid

Hatfield in the Albert Felts murder trial. Police later arrested one of Sid's codefendants and charged him with Staton's murder.

The newly elected Republican governor of West Virginia, Ephraim Morgan—tight with the mine owners and no friend of the miners—sent in more state police to put a lid on the violence in Merrimack, but they proved ineffective. The officers got stuck in the mud, literally, and for hours that afternoon and evening they were pinned down by union snipers. A train carrying more state police came under fire as well. The conductor refused to brake until well past the planned stop for the troopers to get off. When the officers hiked their way back toward the mine camps, they, too, caught the attention of the miners and their guns. More shots rang out, and the state troopers turned tail and ran into the woods, no use to anybody in bringing a halt to the still-raging street battle in Merrimack and the spillover into nearby Matewan, a couple of bends in the river away.

The fighting continued for three days, with as many as twenty killed, though no one could ever say for sure, since many of the dead, at least on the miners' side, were carried out of the woods and buried in secret. In the end, it was a deputy sheriff going to one side of the conflict, and a local doctor, crawling under fire through the woods to the other, who negotiated a truce between the miners and the strikebreakers. District 17 union president Frank Keeney, attempting unsuccessfully to downplay the violence, would later refer to it as "a shooting bee."

The governor took a decidedly different view of the situation and finally declared martial law, ordering all law enforcement in Mingo County to be handled by the state police under the iron-fisted command of Major Thomas B. Davis. Davis had a

long history with the miners: in the Paint Creek–Cabin Creek
strike, he had ordered mass arrests of union leaders, shut down
pro-union and socialist presses, and locked up Mother Jones. To
beef up the police force now, anti-union civic leaders launched
an eight-hundred-member "vigilance committee" made up of the
"better citizens" of Mingo County. Members were issued Winchester rifles from the state armory and put on standby for
whenever they were needed to maintain order, which was code
for keeping close tabs on the striking miners.

On May 19, 1921, exactly one year after the Battle of Matewan, the governor issued an edict making it a crime in Mingo for
anyone besides law enforcement and members of the vigilance
committee to carry a gun, hold a public meeting, or publish anything critical of the government, either West Virginia or US. A
couple of union newspapers were banned almost immediately,
and several striking miners were arrested for reading them. The
Bill of Rights, practically speaking, was suspended in southern
West Virginia. For years, decades even, the miners had been
denied their rights in company-owned towns under the mine-
guard system and the heavy-handed control of the mine owners.
Now, under state-ordered martial law, it was official.

But the violence in Bloody Mingo didn't stop overnight. In
fact, it didn't stop at all. On May 25, snipers hidden in the Kentucky hills were back at it, firing on the Big Splint colliery near
the town of Nolan and killing a state trooper and a guardsman.
When the police arrived, they shot one of the snipers and captured two others, including one they chased into Kentucky and
dragged back over to the West Virginia side of the Tug River.

But that was nothing compared to what happened at Lick

Creek, near Williamson, where a tent colony of striking miners and their families had been living for the past year. On June 5, when a carload of strange men drove by, the miners, thinking the men might be vigilantes, retrieved their hidden rifles and chased off the car in a hail of gunfire. The state police and sheriff responded by swooping into the Lick Creek camp and arresting forty miners, whoever was around, with the threat to lock up even more if there was any further trouble.

Nine days after that, when police showed up again at Lick Creek to arrest yet another miner in yet another shooting incident, the suspect figured to hell with it and started blasting away at them with his pistol. More snipers in the hills soon joined in, no doubt expecting to thwart the arrest. But the state police, with Major Tom Davis himself there on-site, returned fire with one of the new tommy guns they'd recently purchased, tearing up the hillside and keeping the snipers penned down until Davis could summon backup. Backup arrived not long after in the form of seventy members of the "Law and Order Committee," who boxed in the snipers and sealed off all the entrances and exits to the tent colony. Then they attacked, trashing tents, destroying furniture, arresting dozens of men, and leaving their families homeless. One miner, Alex Breedlove, was killed.

Forty-seven miners were crammed into a single jail cell in Williamson and kept there for four days. Eight were ultimately charged with violating martial law. The rest trooped back to Lick Creek to find somewhere for them and their families to live. Alex Breedlove was buried, a martyr to the cause. Hundreds came to his funeral and shared the story—and the outrage— about how he'd been killed. A US senator, sympathetic to the union cause, denounced the killing, mentioning Breedlove by name on the Senate floor, officially the twenty-sixth man to be killed in the southern West Virginia coalfields since the shootout in Matewan.

Meanwhile, word got around that the miners' hero, Sid Hatfield, had been indicted yet again, this time for assaulting a mine supervisor he'd run into while patrolling the streets of Matewan during the Three Days' Battle.

But Major Davis and his state police weren't done just yet. On July 8, Davis led a raid on the union headquarters in Williamson, declaring that the very existence of it was a violation of martial law. Every union

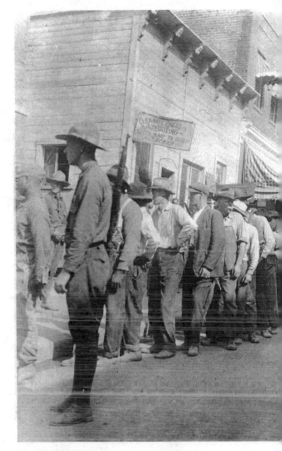

Some of the forty-two miners arrested in the state police raid on the Lick Creek Tent Colony during the strike.

official there at the time and a handful of miners, who'd shown up just looking for a little relief money for their families, were thrown in jail and let out only if they agreed to leave the state.

"The big advantage of this martial law is that if there's an agitator around you can just stick him in jail and keep him there," Davis told a reporter at the time, perhaps explaining why folks soon took to calling him "Emperor of the Tug."

CHAPTER ELEVEN

"We have tried every possible way to end the trouble"

United Mine Workers of America District 17 president Frank Keeney had seen and heard enough. More than a year into the strike, progress was stalled and things were unravelling fast. The mines were operating, many at full capacity, with scab labor, and there was little the striking miners could do about it. Dozens were facing charges, everything from illegal assembly to murder. The union was running low on relief funds and money for legal fees. A story was making the rounds that Keeney himself had been shot down at Lick Creek by Major Davis's state police and the Law and Order Committee, a false rumor that might have led to even more violence if Keeney hadn't acted fast to travel to the area and assure the striking miners that he was still very much alive.

With the strikers handcuffed by the declaration of martial law—which had been challenged successfully by the union in the West Virginia supreme court, to the surprise of everyone, but then, to the surprise of no one, replaced by a legal order from the governor that was, by a different name, martial law all over again—Keeney was all for trying different tactics, anything to further the union cause in general, and the cause of the southern West Virginia coal miners in particular. They needed to sway public opinion in the union's favor, and one way to do that, Keeney and other union officials were convinced, was through an open hearing before the US Senate where they could air their grievances against the mine owners and the politicians of Appalachia.

By the summer of 1921, there'd been enough newspaper coverage of the violence and the struggles and the suffering of the strikers' families in West Virginia to make it a national concern. And when union officials persuaded California senator Hiram Johnson to call for an official inquiry, he and his colleagues passed Senate Resolution 80, the title of which was a mouthful: "Directing the Committee on Education and Labor to Investigate the

US Senator Hiram Johnson from California was one of the few national politicians who supported the union movement. He launched the Senate hearings into working conditions for West Virginia miners and violence in the coalfields.

Recent Acts of Violence in the Coal Fields of West Virginia and Adjacent Territory and the Causes which Led to the Conditions which Now Exist in Said Territory."

The hearing date was set for July 14, 1921.

When the gavel came down to start the committee proceedings, the owners took the floor first—and they came out firing. The UMWA, they said, was "an organized band of robbers" who wanted nothing less than to take over ownership of the mines. "Every single solitary disturbance, every murder, every assassination that has been committed in the coal industry in West Virginia is traceable directly to this announced policy of this organization to unionize first and then own the property themselves," a representative of the Williamson Coal Mine Owners Association told the senators.

Miners were already well paid, the owners contended, earning up to $700 a month. As proof that the union no longer represented the majority of the mine workers, an owners' association spokesman said that of the 2,600 who'd gone out on strike a year ago, all but about five hundred had returned to work. He went on to document what the owners claimed were 125 acts of vandalism and violence, and the murders of twenty-seven men— five of them law enforcement officers shot in ambush. Despite all that, the mines were back operating close to capacity—96 percent, the owners claimed—producing 450,000 tons of coal a month.

Union witnesses disputed it all: the production levels, the number of men still out on strike, the pay—which they said was at most $1,000 a year, and that was during the war years, a far cry from any $700 a month. The biggest fiction of all, they insisted, was who the owners alleged was responsible for the violence.

"We have tried every possible way to end the trouble by conciliation," a union lawyer testified. "The operators on the other hand imported what are known in the vernacular of the country as gun men, to terrorize and intimidate people that were returning to work, to break up their organization. Today a condition obtains in Mingo County that has no parallel even in Soviet Russia, or any land in the world."

The union witnesses kept pressing, wanting to talk about the denial of basic rights of self-governance, free assembly, and union representation. But the owners' lawyers insisted on turning the questioning back to the armed conflict. They brought in two witnesses, former union members, who said they'd been summoned under cover of darkness back in July 1920 to join dozens of other striking miners to launch a mass sniper assault on the Freeburn mine, several bends south on the Tug River from Matewan—a charge the union representatives denied.

District 17 treasurer Fred Mooney spent hours before the committee, walking them through all the ways the union had sought a peaceful resolution to the conflicts with the owners, citing meetings, letters, attempted negotiations, filling up countless pages in the hearing transcript with his testimony over multiple days.

The senators, however, seemed more interested in knowing if he carried a gun.

When Frank Keeney was called in to testify, he was asked

why the union paid to defend its members charged with crimes against the coal operators.

"I say we have the same right to protect our members as the coal operators have to protect the Baldwin-Felts guards," he responded. "You do not suppose that we will permit our members to be annihilated because someone presumes them guilty of some crime?"

Keeney was then asked to account for the supposedly higher number of casualties over the past year and a half among the mine guards and operators and replacement workers than among the miners.

Better aim, was Keeney's answer—though probably not a response that helped the union cause.

"I can explain it this way," he said. "When a real mountaineer of Mingo County shoots twice and don't hit a man you know he is not shooting at you. And the [Baldwin-Felts mine guards] imported in there to do the shooting could not equal that; that is all."

The hearings lasted the better part of two hot summer weeks and included testimony and sworn statements from dozens of witnesses on both sides. Perhaps the most compelling was the union organizer Frank Ingham—identified in the hearing transcript, as were all the handful of Black miners who testified, as "Colored." Ingham calmly told his story about being arrested months before in the Mingo County seat of Williamson but never charged with any crime, then taken from the Williamson jail and driven south into union-hostile McDowell County and the town of Welch. He recounted for the senators what happened at midnight, when the McDowell sheriff turned him over to a carload of white assailants who tied him up and drove him deep into the countryside where they brutally beat him and left him for dead.

And still after that, Ingham proudly testified, he went right back to work for the union helping with the striker relief effort.

▲▲▲

The star witnesses in most observers' eyes—perhaps better described as star-*crossed*—were Sid Hatfield and the Baldwin-Felts spy Charlie Lively.

For all his celebrity back in Matewan and Mingo County, Sid seemed to lose his swagger once he got to Washington, so much so that when he was called to testify, the committee chair, Senator William Kenyon of Iowa, exhorted him to speak louder so his answers could be heard in the sweltering committee room.

Sid was predictably grilled about the Battle of Matewan, and he responded by giving the committee a broad outline of what happened: the arrival of the Baldwin-Felts agents, the evictions, the encounter at the train station. "I went up and told Mr. Felts that I would have to arrest him," Sid said. "He said he would turn the compliment on me, that he had a warrant for me."

Then, Sid explained how things had quickly spiraled out of control. The mayor, Sid's friend Cabell Testerman, said the warrant was bogus, Albert Felts pulled out his gun and shot Testerman, and, as Sid recalled, "Then the shooting started in general."

Sid didn't elaborate much, then or later. No, he hadn't brought any men with him for the arrest. No, he hadn't had time to count the number of shots fired. Yes, he'd married Jessie Testerman shortly after the shootout. Yes, he was now running Cabell Testerman's business. No, he didn't know about any witnesses being killed either before or after the trial. Yes, he'd been indicted for killing Anse Hatfield, so he did suppose there was that. No, he hadn't posed as a gunman for the newspapers. A photographer had just asked him to hold up his two pistols, and so he did. Yes, he'd shot and killed a mine foreman several years before, but was cleared because it was self-defense. Yes, he used to take a drink now and then, but gave it up years ago.

And no, Sid didn't know anything about any new indictment down in McDowell County that he had conspired to blow up a coal tipple there way back in August 1920. "This is the first I heard of it," said Hatfield.

But it wouldn't be the last.

Sid didn't end up being a very helpful witness for the union. But when Charlie Lively took the stand a few days later, he didn't do the owners any favors either, as it turned out.

After forced disclosure by the owners that they'd been paying the salaries of a number of sheriff's deputies in the southern counties—not just a conflict of interest, but also illegal in West Virginia—the senators were determined to find out everything they could about Lively's financial arrangements. For much of his time working for Baldwin-Felts, Charlie Lively had also been employed in the mines, and for a considerable period both in West Virginia and in Colorado, he had served as a paid union organizer as well—and as a union officer and as a delegate to the UMWA state convention.

"At the same time, while you were accepting money from the

miners as their representative and employer, you were really, as you have just said, in truth and in fact, the paid agent of the company that you knew was opposed to the miners?" he was asked. "That is true is it not?"

Lively acknowledged that it was.

The interrogation continued: "If you had disclosed your connection with the detective agency, do you suppose the miners would have let you in there at all?"

"I think they would have turned me over to the undertaker," Lively responded.

After a two-hour grilling on the witness stand, Charlie Lively had had about enough of the committee's questions. And the committee had had about enough of Charlie Lively.

It was generally agreed at the hearing's end that neither side had succeeded in moving the needle measuring public opinion, a deeper loss for the union than it was for the owners.

What came out of it all for Sid Hatfield, after the surprise question about the pending indictment for conspiracy in McDowell County, was a dark premonition.

On the way back to West Virginia, he told his union friends that if he had to go down to the McDowell County Courthouse in Welch to face charges—a short thirty miles from Baldwin-Felts headquarters in Bluefield, and very unfriendly territory for anyone associated with the union—he doubted he'd make it out alive.

CHAPTER TWELVE

"There can be no peace in West Virginia"

Sid Hatfield was wrong about one thing. When he was arrested and taken to Welch two weeks after the Senate hearing, nothing happened—other than him being formally charged in the supposed conspiracy to blow up the coal tipple at the Mohawk Mine, spending a night in jail, and then being released on bond. Thirty-five Mingo County miners were also charged in the conspiracy, based on accusations by more Baldwin-Felts spies. When Sid's wife, Jessie, showed up to post the $2,000 bond, the McDowell sheriff, whose last name was also Hatfield, assured her that he would keep Sid safe when they came back for the trial on August 1, four days later.

Jessie wasn't the only one who was anxious. McDowell County was notorious for being almost as anti-union as Don Chafin's Logan County, which was saying a lot, and Sid's lawyer didn't trust the McDowell sheriff to keep his word, openly telling one state newspaper that there were very real fears that Sid Hatfield would be killed when he went to Welch for the trial.

Sid and Jessie, along with their friends Ed and Sallie Chambers, climbed on board the train from Matewan the morning of Monday, August 1, 1921, at 5:15. They had a single bodyguard with them, an off-duty Mingo County deputy named Jim Kirkpatrick. The train wound along the bank of the Tug River, until, at a stop not far from Welch, the group was surprised to see none other than Charlie Lively get on board. Lively even had the gall to sit down next to Kirkpatrick, the bodyguard. They rode the rest of the way in a strained silence.

The trial wasn't scheduled to start until 10:30, so with a few hours to spare, Sid and Jessie and their friends found a restaurant near the train station and went inside for breakfast. Once again, in came Charlie Lively. His presence was ominous—and it would have been even more so had Sid's party known at the time that the McDowell sheriff, the man who'd promised to keep Sid safe while he was in Welch for the trial, had left town, had in fact left the county altogether for a sudden vacation in Virginia.

After breakfast, Sid, Jessie, the Chamberses, and their bodyguard waited in their lawyer's second-floor hotel room across the street from the courthouse. A 10:30 train whistle would mark the arrival of various witnesses and codefendants and the start of the trial. But good news beat the train: Sid's attorney, C. J. Van Fleet, came in to tell them the judge had agreed to a much friendlier change of venue to Greenbrier County, well to the north. So instead of a trial, today there would be a quick hearing where the judge made it formal, and Sid and Jessie and the Chamberses could catch the next train back to Matewan.

Sid, who figured he could now relax, handed his two pistols to Jessie for safekeeping and then stretched out on the bed. The attorney had said it would be best to leave the weapons at the hotel and pick them up after court. Jessie and Kirkpatrick, the bodyguard, looked out the window, surveying the courthouse lawn just across the street, and, for the third time that morning, saw an all-too-familiar figure.

"There is Mr. Lively," Jessie later recalled Kirkpatrick saying. "He is keeping pretty close track of us this morning, isn't he?"

When 10:30 finally arrived, Sid and his party, along with his attorney, left the hotel, crossing Wyoming Street to the courthouse. Sure enough, Charlie Lively was *still* standing up there on the grassy slope at the top of the steep steps they were about to climb. Half a dozen Baldwin-Felts detectives stood there with

The McDowell County Courthouse, where Sid Hatfield and Ed Chambers faced charges for supposedly dynamiting a coal tipple.

him, all of them armed, all of them also sworn in as McDowell County sheriff's deputies. One was Bill Salter, the detective who had hidden in a trash can the year before in Matewan during the shootout, then made his way to safety across the shallow Tug River over into Kentucky. Another was a man named Buster Pence, well known for advising his fellow detectives on how best to be able to claim self-defense in the event of gunplay during an arrest: "Kill 'em with one gun, and hand 'em another one."

The gray, multistory building rising up behind them looked more like a church than a courthouse with its stone façade, arched windows, and soaring clock tower. The McDowell County Courthouse was already famous as the site where the fabled railroad worker John Hardy had been hung back in 1894—his name and story the title and subject of a famous blues song, still sung today, which he himself was supposed to have written while awaiting his execution.

Sid, Jessie, and Ed and Sallie Chambers mounted the steps, with their bodyguard—the only one carrying a weapon—bringing up the rear. It wouldn't have made any difference if Kirkpatrick had been in the lead, as it turned out. He was outnumbered and outgunned. They all were. "He was poor protection," Jessie Hatfield would testify later. "There were too many men for him. He had to run."

Jessie, Sallie, and C. J. Van Fleet, Sid's attorney, gave the following account of what happened next:

Two flights of stone stairs went up the steep hill to the courthouse lawn. When the Hatfields and the Chamberses reached the landing at the top of the first flight, Sid raised his hand to wave to some friends and said, "Hello, boys." They were his last words.

Charlie Lively, Bill Salter, and Buster Pence, who had walked over to the top of the steps, opened fire.

The first bullet to hit Sid Hatfield caught him in the arm. The second slammed into his chest and spun him around. Two more shots were fired into his back. He fell onto the steps, already dead. Jessie Hatfield turned and ran when the shooting started—down the stairs, down the street to the sheriff's office, the sheriff who had sworn to protect them and who had long since left town.

Ed Chambers, also hit in the first volley, fell back to the middle landing. "My husband, he rolled back down the steps," Sallie Chambers later testified. "I looked down this way and I seen him rolling down and blood gushing from his neck, and I just went back down the steps after him, you see, and they kept on shooting him. . . ."

Lively pushed past the fallen Sid to finish the job on Ed Chambers, ignoring Sallie's pleas for him to stop. "Oh, please, Mr. Lively, don't shoot him anymore. You have killed him now," she begged, just before Lively aimed at the back of Chambers's head at close range and shot him one last time.

Furious, shocked, and grief-stricken, Sallie attacked Lively with an umbrella she was carrying, hitting him over and over until he threatened to shoot her as well. The other Baldwin-Felts men separated them, but Sallie got free and managed to hit Lively once more before he jerked the umbrella away from her and threw it over the steep bank. The last thing Sallie did before the detectives dragged her away was run back to her husband's body to hold him and to show any witnesses close enough to see that he hadn't been carrying any weapons.

"What did you do this for?" Sallie yelled back to Bill Salter as the detectives dragged her away. "We didn't come up here for this."

"Well that is all right," Salter responded. "We didn't come down to Matewan on the 19th of May for this either."

According to the Labor Press, a pro-labor news service, three witnesses to the shooting submitted signed affidavits supporting Sallie's, Jessie's, and the attorney's accounts of the shooting, though they insisted that their names not be used in published reports for fear of reprisal. They said that one of the Baldwin-Felts men fired several bullets into the side of the courthouse to make it appear as if Sid and Ed had shot at them first. They also said a bystander was wounded in the thigh by a stray bullet, but lived, and once Sallie was forcibly spirited away, one of the Baldwin-Felts agents tucked pistols into the still-warm hands of the now dead Sid Hatfield and Ed Chambers.

The McDowell County prosecuting attorney, after examining the eyewitness affidavits, said they corroborated the version of events he'd gotten from Sid's attorney.

The *New York Times*, like a lot of papers, ran a front-page story saying that Sid and Ed had been armed and had shot at the Baldwin-Felts detectives. "One of the guns carried by Hatfield—witnesses said he carried two—had been discharged, it was said by those who rushed forward," the *Times* reported, relying heavily on passive construction to make up for the fact that no sources were cited anywhere in the article. Perhaps because the only ones who "rushed forward" were the Baldwin-Felts men, who immediately cordoned off the bodies from onlookers. "All chambers in the pistol were empty, it was said," the *Times* article continued. "It was stated further that Chambers had only one gun, some of the shells in which had been fired."

Charlie Lively, to no one's surprise, claimed he'd acted in self-defense.

"I happened to look down the steps and there stood Sid Hatfield, Ed Chambers and their wives on the first landing," he said in an interview a few days later with the Associated Press. "They were looking at me and exchanged glances, nodding their heads. Sid said something to Ed I couldn't hear. Suddenly they stepped apart. I could see Sid's jaws set like a steel trap. Both men pulled their guns; as they did so I jumped to my feet and pulled mine. Sid fired at me and I immediately shot back. I had two pistols and was using both. Sid staggered and fell, as did Chambers immediately afterwards. Then Mrs. Chambers attacked me with her umbrella. I grabbed the umbrella, threw it away and then walked over to the office of A. C. Hufford, justice of the peace, and surrendered. The report that I shot into Chambers' body while he was lying on the steps dead is an absolute lie."

The part about the umbrella was true, anyway.

Tom Felts showed up in Welch the afternoon of the shooting with $3,000 to post bail for the three Baldwin-Felts men. And a little more than a year after the Matewan Massacre, Tom Felts and the Baldwin-Felts Detective Agency had their revenge.

It was raining two days later when the bodies of Sid and Ed were brought back to Matewan on the early morning train. The Tug River was full and running fast. Two thousand people crowded the town, mostly miners and their families, all under the watchful eyes of state police and the anti-union Law and Order Committee's Matewan Militia. Mingo County was still ruled by martial law, so the heads of UMWA District 17—Frank Keeney and Fred Mooney—stayed away in Charleston to keep from being arrested. All morning the next day, August 4, folks stopped by the Chambers and Hatfield homes to view the open coffins and pay their respects. In the afternoon, a long line of mourners followed the pallbearers over a trembling suspension bridge across the Tug and back to Kentucky near where Sid was born. There was a short graveside service for the two slain men. A minister spoke. The rain continued, now coming down in heavy sheets.

The union lawyer Sam Montgomery, once a candidate for West Virginia governor, gave the eulogy. "We have gathered here today to perform the last sad rites for these two boys who fell victims to one of the most contemptible systems that has

Jessie Hatfield and Sallie Chambers at a US Senate hearing after the murders of their husbands.

ever been known to exist in the history of the so-called civilized world," he told the crowd of mourners. It was a system run by "sleek, dignified churchgoing gentlemen who would rather pay fabulous sums to their hired gunmen, to kill and slay men for joining a union, than to pay like or less amounts to the men who delve into the subterranean depths of the earth and produce their wealth for them. . . .

"There can be no peace in West Virginia," he said, "until the enforcement of the laws is removed from the hands of private detective agencies and from those of deputy sheriffs who are paid, not by the state, but by the great corporations, most of them owned by non-residents who have no interest in West Virginia's tomorrow."

The rain never let up as Montgomery finished his eulogy. "Even the heavens weep with the grief-stricken relatives and bereaved friends of these two boys," he concluded, and neither did the sorrow and the anger throughout the coal towns of southern West Virginia.

Charlie Lively, meanwhile, was sitting down with a reporter back in Welch, holding forth in an interview for a sympathetic profile.

"My work is my love," he said with obvious pride. "When I made friends with Sid Hatfield and his bunch, I put my whole heart and soul in it. My work is chiefly a matter of auto-suggestion. When I talk to and associate with people from whom I want information, or on whom I want to 'get' something, I talk myself into a rock-like conviction that I actually am their friend. I forget all about being a detective. I clear my mind, my whole conscious self, of every atom of realization of my real identity.

Thus, I quickly begin to sympathize with them, earnestly and sincerely, I share their joys and sorrows, I am for them heart and souls. Not until my day—or night, for I do much night work—is all ended and I am alone in my room do I remember that I had an ulterior motive, that I have been 'working.' Then I lock the door, pull down the shade, take my pad and pencil and write my report to headquarters."

He didn't have much more to say about the killings. The doctor who examined the bodies later determined that Sid Hatfield had been shot six times, Ed Chambers eight.

CHAPTER THIRTEEN

"Primitive ferocities"

The United Mine Workers Journal made no bones about it: "Never in the history of the country did a cold-blooded murder ever create as much indignation as the double murder of Sid Hatfield and Ed Chambers," they wrote.

The story made headlines all over the country. The newspaper in Wheeling, West Virginia, called it "the most glaring and outrageous expression of contempt for law that has ever stained the history of West Virginia."

The nearby Bluefield, West Virginia, *Daily Telegraph* took a different tack and tried to wax poetic about Sid Hatfield's final end: "Those who saw the bodies of Hatfield and Chambers after the two men had been shot at the court house entrance positively asserted that the smile of the Matewan ex-chief of police remained even in death. That smile has been the subject dwelt

Tuesday, August 2, 1921.

TERRORISM INSTEAD OF LAW

The shooting of Sid Hatfield and Ed Chambers on the steps of the courthouse at Welch yesterday was the most glaring and outrageous expression of contempt for the law that has ever stained the history of West Virginia. These two men had been charged with an offense and were at first unwilling to go to Welch, as threats had been made against their lives, especially that of Hatfield. Finally, on the advice of influential friends, who believed that they should comply with the law and that the law in return would protect them, Hatfield and Chambers entered the dangerous territory.

Their hearing had been set for yesterday, and while they were on the steps of the courthouse they were inveigled into a controversy and shot dead almost at the threshold of the temple of justice. This is the climax of the reign of lawlessness that has prevailed in the coal fields of southern West Virginia for some time.

It is the direct outgrowth and one of the many bloody incidents of the iniquitous private mine guard and private detective system which have been the curse of the coal fields for years. As long as this system exists, we may expect just such contempt for the law and just such tragedies.

Except for the treachery of a few men in high places, the private mine guards and detectives would have been abolished at the last session of the state legislature. The Republican party had given a pledge to the people of this state in its platform to abolish the system. The proper bill was introduced in good faith in the state senate. It was reported by the judiciary committee and brought out on the floor. What happened then may be best told in the words of Senator Bloch:

"It could not have been defeated from the floor of either house, but the coal interests were against its passage. They feared the loss of their political control in the counties where the mine guard system is most flagrantly in force, and accordingly brought pressure to bear upon the governor. He in turn passed it on to his chief advisers and supporters in the senate, and succeeded in having the bill taken back to the committee room under pretense that an amendment was to be offered. The mine guard bill died there. It was tabled in the committee room and never again mentioned."

Sid Hatfield and Ed Chambers were killed yesterday by men who formed a part of the mine guard system. The Matewan tragedy, in which ten men died, was another slaughter directly due to this same bloodstained cause. Similar crimes will continue to blacken the fair name of our state until the people rise in righteous wrath and demand that these hired thugs of the coal interests be forever wiped out.

The *Wheeling Intelligencer* reported the murder of Sid Hatfield and Ed Chambers under the headline "Terrorism Instead of Law."

upon by all who came in contact with Hatfield and earned for him the sobriquet of 'Smilin' Sid.'"

The *Fort Wayne Journal Gazette* saw little chance of there being a fair trial in the aftermath of the killings. "When Hatfield and Chambers went into Welch, W.V., they went into an 'unfriendly' county, McDowell, where the Felts men are strong. If it is true, as Tom Felts said, that no jury in Mingo will ever convict the Matewan accused, it is equally safe to say that it will be difficult to find a jury in McDowell county to convict Lively."

A few months after the shooting—despite the eyewitness testimony, and even with a change of venue out of McDowell County for the trial—Charlie Lively, Bill Salter, and Buster Pence were acquitted of the murders of Sid Hatfield and Ed Chambers.

But outside the state, the murders were viewed through the lens of pervasive stereotypes about West Virginia, seen as little more than a violent, uncultured backwater where blood feuds had gone on forever and just seemed to keep happening. In a snide editorial, the *New York Times* suggested that only when the last feuding mountaineer perished would there ever be peace in the Mountain State.

"Hatfields and McCoys are as famous in the West Virginia mountains as ever Armstrongs and Eliots were on the Scotch border," the *Times* wrote in their editorial headlined "The Primitive Mountaineer." "They carry on clan feuds in the ancient way. Sometimes they do a little outside shooting from habit or to keep their hand in. They are a curious survival, a sixteenth century fauna flourishing in the twentieth. They are of the days before the law. They wage private war. For the rest, often good-natured folk, simple, religious, or at least given to religious observances, a little careless with firearms, but, save for their primitive ferocities, probably not essentially worse than most other people.

"Sid, a pleasant young chap of 26, sometimes the spirited Matewan Chief of Police, perished in no tribal combat. He must have felt himself [fated to die] ever since he was acquitted of the charge of murder a few months ago. There had been a pretty popping of guns at Matewan, and eleven men were killed. He must have felt that he wasn't a good risk when he came to Welch to be tried for his part in a mining hamlet shooting scrape last year. The trial has been postponed indefinitely. Sid and a companion were killed in front of the Court House. Who fired the first shot, after a short parley, amicable at first, isn't made clear; but perhaps the private detective Lively acted his name. Surely, if Sid had got the 'draw,' an artist of his experience would have made full use of it. The good behavior of the crowd of mountaineers deserves a kind word. There was none of that neurotic excitement which would have blazed up in communities of ordinary heredity.

"It was an orderly, quiet and successful shooting match. That it took place in the shadow of a court house needn't prompt us to any obvious moralizing or special virtuous indignation. These men are of an inheritance and habit apart. Only slow Time can cure them. Meanwhile Time is not so slow in killing off their most active specimens."

The sentiment, and the language, were as offensive then as they are today but show how little support the miners of West Virginia had at the time, reaffirming what they had always known: that if things were ever going to change in coal country, the miners themselves—and their union—would have to be the ones to make it happen. Two of their own had just been murdered in cold blood, in public, by Baldwin-Felts men doubling as deputy sheriffs, protected by all the official powers that be in West Virginia, from town to county to state, with the coal mine owners and operators behind it all, pulling the strings. Meanwhile, hundreds of striking miners sat in jail, many of them arrested for violations of martial law so minor they still weren't sure what crimes they were accused of committing. Reading a union pamphlet? Gathering with more than one other person? Cursing at scabs?

The District 17 leaders—Keeney and Mooney—were at their wits' end. They wanted to launch a civil disobedience campaign in the southern counties to protest the killings of Sid Hatfield and Ed Chambers. Maybe that would finally pressure the governor to protect the striking workers from the mine guards, or even order the Baldwin-Felts men out of the coalfields altogether. But they were also worried about more of their own being killed. Getting sent to jail was one thing; bodies sent home in coffins—with no repercussion for the ones who put them there—was another. Maybe what the union needed, instead, was a cooling-off period for the striking miners, many of whom were already reported to be arming themselves for their own revenge.

But Mother Jones, who'd been in and out of West Virginia throughout the past year, had another idea. To hell with all this talk of everybody stepping back from the conflict, she told the union leaders. Now was the time to protest, to make demands, to let 'em know the miners of West Virginia were mad as hell and they weren't going to take it anymore. A few days after Sid and Ed were laid to rest, Mother Jones stormed into Charleston to organize a mass "Indignation Rally" at the state fairgrounds, joined by Keeney and Mooney, to be followed by a march over to the governor's office with a list of demands:

AN END TO MARTIAL LAW IN MINGO COUNTY.

Release of all union members from the Mingo County jail.

An end to the mine guard system, and punitive action against the Baldwin-Felts Detective Agency.

Official condemnation of the murders of Sid Hatfield and Ed Chambers—and condemnation of the man most responsible for their deaths, one Charles E. Lively, being let out on bail.

And a joint labor-management commission to negotiate wages and mediate disputes between coal operators and miners.

By one account, 5,000 miners and supporters showed up at the fairgrounds. By another account, there were only five hundred, and the governor, Ephraim Morgan, hardly knew they were there. There were also mixed reports about what was said. In a couple of versions, Frank Keeney, though cautious before, threw caution to the wind and called for armed resistance. The governor had refused to call off martial law, he said. "Therefore, you have no recourse except to fight. The only way you can get your rights is with a high-power rifle, and the man who does not have this equipment is not a good union man."

Mother Jones, once again in failing health with worsening rheumatism, wasn't altogether coherent, sometimes rambling through her speeches in those later years. She'd had a correspondence going for a while with Governor Morgan, who'd taken office in March, and she seemed to think she could talk him into doing the right thing for the miners. Keeney and Mooney weren't convinced that the governor would be receptive to the union's demands, but there was nothing else they could think to do that might stop what already seemed poised to turn into an all-out war.

Governor Morgan took the meeting with Mother Jones and a reluctant Keeney and Mooney—despite another report that Mother Jones, in her hour-long speech at the fairgrounds, had called him "a tool of the [expletive] coal operators." He listened to their demands, said he'd take them under advisement, then sat on everything for a week and a half while the miners stewed. After those ten days, he rejected it all out of hand. No end to martial law. No halt to the mine guard system. No reprimand for Baldwin-Felts. No comment on the murders of Sid and Ed. No coal commission, joint or otherwise.

As far as he was concerned, Morgan said, nobody had done anything wrong. Not the state police, not the mine owners, not the private mine guards—nobody, that is, except these outside agitators from the UMWA, coming into West Virginia stirring up labor trouble in coal country.

It was an old but useful canard, blaming supposed outsiders

for problems in your own backyard, suggesting in this case that, without union organizers whispering in their ears, the miners would have otherwise been happy with whatever the owners gave them. If only these troublemakers hadn't come in from somewhere else and stirred things up! But it was a lie. Aside from Mother Jones, who was herself practically an honorary citizen of West Virginia, all the United Mine Workers organizers and District 17 leaders had been born and raised in the Mountain State. And the problems they were fighting to address in the coalfields of southern Appalachia were all too real.

Even with the still-raw anger and outrage over the McDowell County murders, in the court of public opinion, it probably wasn't a good time for labor to be making public demands with any expectation that the governor, or any politician, would agree to meet them. Not that there would ever be a good time. The Red Scare that had so rocked America for the past two years may have faded in some ways. There were no more anarchist bombings spurring harsh government reprisals, no more roundups and deportations of supposed foreign radicals. The fierce strikes of 1919 and 1920 in the steel and coal industries had largely been settled—or crushed. A police strike in Boston and a general strike in Seattle, both of which had garnered national attention and condemnation, had ended.

But most Americans, their passions inflamed for years by those old newspaper headlines, still reflexively equated the labor movement with Bolshevism and had little sympathy for current strikes in southern West Virginia or anywhere else. Two years before, when the UMWA had called for the nationwide strike that eventually got union mines their promised 14 percent raise, the *New York Tribune* had attacked the miners as being "red-soaked in the doctrines of Bolshevism" and "starting a general revolution in America."

What Frank Keeney and Fred Mooney and Mother Jones didn't know—couldn't have known—was that union numbers nationwide were in a free fall and by the end of the 1920s would drop from a postwar high of five million members down to three million. Little wonder that Governor Morgan fell back on that tried-and-true tactic of blaming those supposed outsiders— unionists, revolutionists, Bolsheviks—for causing all the labor trouble in West Virginia.

Few people, it seemed, were ever going to take a stand on behalf of the miners.

CHAPTER FOURTEEN

"The boys need guns. Act at once"

Even before the governor issued his flat-out rejection of the union demands, angry West Virginia miners had begun to gather in and around the town of Clothier, just north of Don Chafin's Logan County. And they weren't just gathering, but arming themselves and discussing tentative plans of action as well. At first it was just a few dozen. And then a few hundred. The mine owners had murdered Sid Hatfield, and they'd gotten away with it. Hundreds of out-of-work miners were locked up in Mingo County. Somebody had to be held accountable. Somebody had to do *something*.

Already, a confidential letter had gone out from a union attorney to one of the local union officers in the town of Blair recommending money from the union's burial fund be used instead to buy "necessary equipment for the Mingo enterprise." The letter, inadvertently kept in union files and discovered years later,

Armed miners in Kanawha Fields, West Virginia, angry about the assassinations of Sid Hatfield and Ed Chambers.

went on to say, "The boys need guns, etc. Act at once. You can't trust the bearer of this note. Destroy it as soon as read."

It wasn't the first time the miners had armed themselves and threatened a mass insurrection. Two years earlier, in September 1919, 5,000 angry miners with guns had rallied in the town of Marmet, ten miles south of the state capital, so sick of the mine guard system and the brutal control Don Chafin held down in Logan County that they vowed they were going to force their way there and do away with the sheriff once and for all. Earlier that year, Mother Jones had sent two union organizers into Logan with instructions to be as secretive about what they were up to as possible. But Don Chafin found out they were in his county anyway, a witness later recalled, and had them picked up by his deputies and taken to a remote site on Blair Mountain where he intended to kill them, until one of his deputies intervened. "Don, you can pistol whip them if you want, but I don't think it would be a good idea to kill them," the deputy said.

So that was what they did.

Locals called it "Chafin justice." And more brutality against union organizers, or anyone so much as speaking out in support of the union, followed. That chief clerk of the mines department who was mistaken for a union organizer. A Black minister who dared to preach a pro-union sermon. A miner who refused to spy on his coworkers. Those fifty organizers Frank Keeney hired to flood the mining towns back in 1919. All were beaten, threatened, forced out of Logan County.

The governor at the time, John J. Cornwell, had promised when he ran for office that he would rein in the mine guards, but he'd never followed through. When he got word of the miners' plan for an all-out assault on Logan County in 1919, he drove to Marmet in the middle of the night, and to his credit climbed onto the hood of his car to address the gun-toting mob amid their campfires and tents. "It looked more like Dante's Inferno than anything I can think of with the moonlight shining on the rifles," Frank Keeney recalled. He and Fred Mooney echoed the plea for restraint, but the miners shouted them all down. Cornwell scurried back to the capital and called in federal troops, while at the same time promising to create a commission to study the mine guard problem and make recommendations for reform— not that anybody expected much to come of it, and not that anything did.

The 5,000 miners stood down. That time.

But from the looks of things now, two years later, they weren't going to stand down again.

And almost as if to make certain of it, on Friday, August 12, while Governor Ephraim Morgan was supposedly still mulling over the union demands, five mounted state police rode their horses into Clothier in what was intended to be a show of force. Don Chafin had gotten wind of the miners gathering north of Logan County, and, nervous about their growing numbers, he had asked for help from the state. What he got instead was a clown show. One of the riders crashed his horse into a parked car and fell off. The other troopers, embarrassed, dragged the innocent driver out of the vehicle, roughed him up, and then let him go.

Word quickly got back to the group congregated just outside Clothier. Several rushed over to confront the troopers, but when they couldn't find them, the miners instead shot up another car that just happened to be passing by—wrong place, wrong time. The driver escaped unharmed and sped off to Logan County, where he told Don Chafin about the attack. A carload of deputies and state police was then sent *back* to Clothier to investigate—and was immediately surrounded by a swarm of miners who ordered the troopers out of their vehicle, confiscated their weapons, and forced them to hightail it out of town on foot. The miners then blockaded all the roads, cut telegraph and phone lines, and waited to see how the governor would respond to the union demands.

Little physical harm was done to either side—a few bumps and bruises, half a dozen bullet holes but no casualties—but in time, the dustup in Clothier would come back to haunt everyone who was there that day, and thousands more besides.

While all this was going on, a young union organizer named Savoy Holt was crisscrossing the state like mad, carrying a letter from Frank Keeney urging every union local all up and down the Kanawha Coal Field and beyond to meet up in the town of Marmet, just up the road from Clothier. They were planning another mass march, even larger this time, from Marmet south to Mingo County, a fifty-mile trek over Blair Mountain that would take them straight through the heart of Logan County. If Don Chafin decided to get in the way, well, they'd just have to deal with him. And once they got to Mingo, the miners would do whatever was necessary to set free the hundreds still in jail there on those bogus charges under martial law.

To cover himself, Keeney disavowed the letter Savoy Holt was distributing, though few doubted he was in fact in on the planning for the march. "I wash my hands of the whole affair," he told the *New York Times*. That was on August 19, a week after the craziness in Clothier. "I've interfered time and again to stop such enterprises. I seem to have halted them only temporarily. This time they can march to Mingo, so far as I am concerned."

In quick succession, the governor rejected the union demands, and the state supreme court announced that it was also rejecting the union's legal challenge to the declaration of martial law. Almost overnight, those six hundred miners in Clothier turned into 6,000, pouring into nearby Marmet on foot, in cars, on flatbed trucks, on tops of trains. Unionized mines all over the state shut down for lack of workers. Wild rumors flew everywhere, many of them reported in the West Virginia newspapers: the miners were out of control, robbing people left and right, blocking the roads, hell-bent on wanton destruction, the pandemonium fueled by what Governor Morgan said were the three evils of "moonshine liquor, pistol-toting, and automobiles."

Folks in the state capital, just ten miles north of the miners' spreading encampment in Marmet, were on high alert, worried that the attack, when it came, would be aimed their way. But the miners' focus was unwavering: they weren't heading to Charleston. Who cared about Charleston? The politicians could all go to hell, as far as they were concerned. No, where they were marching, once they got the signal, was straight south—down to Mingo. And along the way they had those other plans, which they sang to the tune of "John Brown's Body": "We'll hang Don Chafin to a sour apple tree!"

Chafin, meanwhile, was busy amassing an army of his own, adding to his "Standing Army of Logan" a host of new volunteers whom he listed by their professions: "Lawyers, bankers, preachers, doctors and farmers." There were 250 American Legion members from Welch. A handful of high school ROTC kids from Charleston. A contingent of six hundred volunteers from McDowell County led by the sheriff, William Hatfield, the man who had promised to protect Sid Hatfield but had instead gone on vacation in Virginia to take the waters, as was sometimes said. Chafin also forced hundreds of nonunion miners to sign up or risk losing their jobs if they refused. He even emptied the jails to fill his many defensive assignments—chopping down trees, digging trenches, building breastworks, barricading roads, shoring up defenses all along the ridge of Blair Mountain.

"No armed mob will cross Logan County," Chafin swore. And then he set about emptying the county armory and every gun and hardware store in the area to make sure his army, now swollen to more than 3,000, had the weapons and ammunition to back up his vow.

Plus there were three biplanes at the ready on the local baseball field, because you just never knew when you might need them for surveillance, or to drop a few bombs.

As quickly as Chafin's army was growing, the miners' side was growing even faster. By August 24, observers had bumped up the estimate again—to 10,000 armed and deeply agitated miners in Marmet, working themselves into a frenzy, thirsting for revenge, ready to do battle. They even had uniforms of a sort: blue bib overalls and red bandannas, leading people, themselves included, to refer to them as the Redneck Army. On the other side of Blair Mountain, Don Chafin's soldiers took to wearing proper khakis and wide-brimmed hats, just like a regular army, plus white armbands to distinguish themselves from the Reds, as they called the miners. So it was to be the Reds vs. the Whites.

Some on both sides, veterans of the Great War, pulled out their old American Expeditionary Forces uniforms and wore them instead. And if they still had their army-issued rifles, they pulled those out, too.

From what Mother Jones could see and hear, this wasn't

going to end well for the miners. Or for anybody. Don Chafin had machine guns. The miners had gotten their hands on at least one Gatling gun. The governor was calling for federal intervention— and the president, Warren Harding, was considering the request. Two weeks earlier, Mother Jones had been one of the loudest and most profane voices calling for action, even militant action, against the mine owners. At least rhetorically. But her fear now was that things had spiraled too far out of control and would end in a bloodbath and Armageddon for her boys.

So she contacted Frank Keeney and Fred Mooney and said she was going out to Marmet, to where Lens Creek flowed into the Kanawha River, to deliver a message to the assembled pro-testers—a surprise telegram she'd just received from Presi-dent Warren Harding himself. Keeney and Mooney, nervous about what Mother Jones might be up to, raced down to Lens Creek from Charleston to head her off at the pass. They didn't believe for a second that there was any such telegram from the president.

Mother Jones was already there when they arrived, standing on the side of a hill, surrounded by the teeming army of angry miners. Guns were everywhere. Keeney and Mooney didn't have any choice but to let her speak.

Mother Jones held up a piece of paper. They needed to call off the march, she told the men gathered tightly around her. They couldn't win and ought to go home. And if they did, Presi-dent Harding—whose telegram she had in her hand at that very moment—promised he would take up their cause.

"I request that you abandon your purpose and return to your homes," Mother Jones read, "and I assure you that my good offices will be used to forever eliminate the gunman system from the state of West Virginia."

Like Mother Jones, Mooney and Keeney were both worried about the threatened violence getting out of hand and backfiring, but deceiving the miners was the wrong way to try to protect them.

So Fred Mooney stepped forward and denounced the telegram as a lie.

Mother Jones told him to go to hell, that it was none of his business.

Keeney demanded to see the telegram and reached out to take it. It didn't sound like something President Harding had written. This was, after all, the same president whose speeches were once described as "an army of pompous phrases moving across the landscape in search of an idea."

Reads Fake Telegram.

Charleston, W. Va., Aug. 25.—C. F. Keeney, president of District 18, United Mine Workers of America, issued a statement here today denying reports current during the day that the men assembled at Marmet had taken a vote to disperse and return to their homes.

Keeney also took occasion to say in his statement that a telegram purporting to have come from President Harding, and which he said had been read to the men today by "Mother" Jones, labor organizer, was bogus. The union president said that he and Fred Mooney, secretary of the organization, had gone to the camp on request of the men, where they heard "Mother" Jones read the telegram purporting to have come from the president, asking the men to return to their homes and stating that he would use his influence to drive guards of a detective agency from the State.

Keeney said "Mother" Jones refused to show him the telegram and that upon his return to Charleston he obtained information from President Harding's secretary by long distance telephone that no telegram had been sent.

Small groups of armed men straggled into the camp today, according to Sheriff Walker, of Kanawha county, who said that he estimated there were more than 5,000 men now assembled at Marmet.

Fight Among Selves.

As tensions ratcheted up in southern West Virginia, the *Martinsburg Journal* reported on the "bogus" telegram Mother Jones had read aloud to the miners.

Plus, everybody knew Harding was no friend of the miners. His campaign slogan had been, "Less government in business and more business in government."

Mother Jones snatched the paper away and told Keeney to go to hell, too.

Keeney turned to the crowd of bewildered and now suspicious miners. "Well, boys," he said, "that telegram is a fake, so is Mother Jones. We will just move on."

A furious Mother Jones retreated. Keeney and Mooney raced back to Charleston to confirm their suspicions about the telegram. Word quickly came back from the White House that the president wasn't even in Washington at the time and certainly hadn't sent any such message.

And the march to Mingo was on.

Mother Jones, who'd been fighting for workers' rights in West Virginia for a quarter of a century, would only return to the state one more time—to lobby for the release of imprisoned miners. But her credibility with the union was now shot through with holes. She'd had the best interests of her boys at heart—possibly she was afraid they were walking into a trap—but she'd gone too far in thinking she'd be taken at her word by the union leaders about the message from the president.

What came out later, further undermining her standing with the miners, were back-channel communications she'd been having with Governor Morgan, who convinced her that he, too, had the workers' best interests at heart—this despite his harsh rejection of literally every single one of the union's demands and his placing responsibility for the insurrection on those supposed "outsiders."

Just as many of the miners never forgave Mother Jones, Mother Jones never forgave the union leaders, Frank Keeney and Fred Mooney, whom she'd mentored over the years and had loved as if they were her own children.

Ironically, eight days later, President Harding would do exactly what Mother Jones falsely claimed he'd already done—issue an appeal, actually more of an executive order at that point, for the miners' army to cease and desist. Don Chafin's biplanes would drop thousands of leaflets over the marchers with Harding's call for them to stand down. But by then it would be way too little and way too late, the miners having already launched their assault on Logan County and the bullets already flying.

CHAPTER FIFTEEN

"An army of malcontents"

The march started in the hot dead of night on August 25 from the miners' encampment in Marmet, several raw hours after the debacle with Mother Jones. A company of six hundred men led the way, with the thousands behind them following along, organized by their union locals. Officially, nobody was in charge. The march just sort of happened. Unofficially, District 17 vice president Bill Blizzard was the "generalissimo" of the Redneck Army, as others took to calling him. Twenty-eight, a second-generation union man, hotheaded in the best of times, Blizzard was wise enough to rely on the military training and experience of significant numbers of his men to lead the companies that formed up out of the locals. But from the very start it was clear that any authority they managed to establish was going to be shaky at best.

When daylight came and one of Don Chafin's biplanes flew

UMWA vice president Bill Blizzard was considered the "generalissimo" of the Redneck Army.

over to get a read on the marchers, dozens of men opened up with their rifles and chased the pilot away. Even darker—a lot darker—was the report that four miners were killed, possibly by other miners, in separate incidents for disobeying orders or refusing to take part in the insurrection.

There were similar reports from the other side as well—a prisoner in Logan County who refused to join Chafin's defenders was subsequently shot and killed. The official reason given: trying to escape.

In contrast to the miners, everybody knew who the undisputed leader was in the Standing Army of Logan. Chafin had his well-armed militia set up a fifteen-mile defensive line along the mountain ridge on the border of Logan and Boone Counties, figuring the slowly advancing miners would try to shoot through one or more of several gaps. Of particular worry was the dirt road that ran between the two 1,900-foot peaks of Blair Mountain. If Chafin's defenders couldn't hold there, it would give the Redneck Army a clear route down the other side of the mountain and straight into the town of Logan.

The miners had about forty miles of rough road to travel just to reach the base of Blair Mountain and the small mining towns of Sharples and Blair, though some were able to hitch rides there on a hijacked train. In preparation for the coming assault, Blizzard's lieutenants issued passwords that would mean the difference between safe passage through friendly lines or getting yourself killed. If anybody asked, "Where are you going?" the only correct answer was "To Mingo." And the response to the challenge, "How are you coming?" was "I come creeping."

The *New York Times* reported that they were an "army of malcontents" whose destination was Mingo County—"union miners, radical organizers and not a few ex servicemen." Together, they were formidable enough to have the governor begging yet again for the president to send troops, planes, and guns to put down the growing threat of mass violence.

President Harding spent the night mulling over the request. An indecisive man in the best of circumstances—and a president who would die in office from a bad heart before finishing out his term—Harding and his advisers chose instead to send Major General Harry Bandholtz, a war hero who had led US forces into battle against the Germans, to use his influence and the threat of federal intervention to convince the miners to halt their advance, put down their weapons, and go home.

As it turned out, Bandholtz wasn't the only war hero making the trek over to Charleston the next day. The other, WWI ace pilot Billy Mitchell, flew into the city's airfield on August 26, 1921, to great fanfare as a large crowd rushed out to greet him, though nobody had asked him to come—and Bandholtz wasn't at all happy that he was there. While Bandholtz carried the weight of grave responsibility to try to stop a war, Mitchell, a publicity hound who, weirdly, was wearing spurs on his boots when he dismounted from his plane, seemed more inclined to fan the flames.

US President Warren G. Harding ordered the armed mine workers to stand down. They ignored him.

When asked how he would deal with the miners, he didn't hesitate. "Gas," he said. "You understand we wouldn't try to kill these people at first. We'd drop tear gas all over the place. If they refused to disperse then we'd open up with artillery. . . ."

Meanwhile, Frank Keeney and Fred Mooney were lying low in Charleston, steering clear of the march now crossing Boone County en route to Logan. The Boone County sheriff had declared he was taking a totally hands-off approach to the Redneck Army, even as they stormed through every company store in every mining camp along the way, sweeping the shelves clean of foodstuffs—and any guns and ammo and dynamite they could find. The way Keeney and Mooney saw it, better to let their fellow West Virginians, and especially the mine owners and the politicians, think it was a leaderless mob with a mind of its own. Publicly, Keeney had already disavowed the whole affair, and he hoped that staying away would more effectively keep the pressure on the governor and the powers that be to offer some sort of compromise before things spiraled completely out of hand.

But General Bandholtz, the president's emissary, wasn't buying it for one second. As soon as he arrived in Charleston, he summoned the two District 17 leaders and read them the riot act. "You two are the officers of this organization and these are your people," he told them straight up. "I am going to give you a chance to save them, and if you cannot turn them back, we are going to snuff this out just like that." He snapped his fingers at them and then went on to make it abundantly clear that he wasn't about to let this labor insurrection continue and risk turning into a general revolution all across America.

"This will never do," he snarled. "There are several million unemployed in this country right now and this thing might assume proportions that would be difficult to handle."

So if they knew what was good for them—and for those 10,000 miners thinking they were going to cut off the head of Don Chafin—Keeney and Mooney better stomp this fire out now.

It must have been a sight to see—the major general and a handful of aides crammed into a couple of Model Ts with the two men assumed to be the leaders of the miners' rebellion, bouncing down West Virginia rutted dirt roads, desperately trying to catch up to the Redneck Army. They'd been in meetings since way before dawn and hit the road early on their joint peace mission, worried about how far things had already gotten. But catch up they did, at the halfway point between Charleston and Logan, in the town of Madison at the mouth of the Little Coal River.

"Mandatory union meeting at the ballfield this afternoon," Keeney and Mooney told the milling crowd before hopping back in the car to chase down the vanguard of a few hundred faster-moving miners. This was no longer about taking out Don Chafin, or getting revenge for the murder of Sid Hatfield, or freeing the union men in Mingo who were still stuck in jail. This was about the president of the United States threatening to send in the US Army if the miners didn't stand down. And nobody, Keeney and Mooney said, wanted any part of that fight. They were Americans, too, after all. They hated the coal operators, the mine guard system, the rigged politics of West Virginia, but they loved their country more.

Keeney was the principal speaker. "I've told you men, God knows how many times, that any time you want to do battle against Don Chafin and his thugs, I'll be right there in the front lines with you," he said. "I've been there before and you know it. But this time you've got more than Don Chafin against you. You've got more than the governor of West Virginia against you. You got the government of the United States against you!

"Now I'm telling you for your own good and for the good of the cause and you've got to do it. Break up this march. Go home. Get back to your jobs. . . . You can fight the government of West Virginia, but, by God, you can't fight the government of the United States."

Leery of being played as they had been by Mother Jones, the miners demanded proof that the message was legitimate. And this time they had their proof in the person of Major General Harry Bandholtz himself, standing right there in front of them that afternoon at the ballfield, recognized as the real deal by former soldiers who'd served under him in the war, confirming every word from Keeney and Mooney.

Bandholtz also confirmed that Governor Morgan had promised to send special trains down from Charleston to carry the miners home, any of those who needed transportation. Keeney exhorted the crowd to spread the word to the rest of the miners who hadn't been able to squeeze onto the bleachers: *either find your own way home or sit tight until the trains arrive.*

So the miners stood down, having hit what appeared to be an insurmountable roadblock. The march ground to a halt.

Word spread quickly through southern West Virginia, even over Blair Mountain to Don Chafin's redoubt. The *Logan Banner*

West Virginia Governor Ephraim Morgan and Major General Harry Bandholtz confer on how to respond to the threat of a miners' march on Logan County.

ran a story with the all-caps headline "ATTEMPTED INVASION FAILS." General Bandholtz went back to Charleston, and from there, after reassuring the governor that all was calm—and urging him to send in those special trains right away—Bandholtz returned to Washington to brief the president.

And that's where it might have ended. Maybe even should have ended. If not for the incendiary actions of the miners' mortal enemy, Logan County sheriff Don Chafin, and the behind-the-scenes conniving of a union man named Bad Lewis White.

Bad Lewis, who by all accounts lived up to his nickname, was as militant a union man as there was. Born, appropriately enough, on Hell Creek down in Mingo County, Bad Lewis had been working in a coal mine near Logan when the insurrection started. And once it did, he wasn't about to let it end, no matter what the District 17 union leaders had to say. As soon as Keeney and Mooney called for a halt to the march, maybe even while they were doing it, Bad Lewis got busy lobbying his fellow miners to keep it going.

The volatile Lewis quickly drew a vocal band of followers and wasn't above threatening anyone who got in their way. Few were interested in challenging him directly, partly because of his violent reputation, partly because he carried a brace of Smith and Wesson pistols, and partly because there was already considerable forward momentum and growing distrust of the union leaders.

"A regular son of a bitch he was," said one of his relatives about Bad Lewis White. "Mean as a snake."

As soon as Fred Mooney caught wind of Bad Lewis's rabble-rousing, he did his best to shut it down. It didn't go well.

"What the hell you fellows mean by stopping these marchers?" White demanded to know.

Mooney said he and Keeney were worried the insurrection could end in slaughter, especially if the feds got involved.

To which Bad Lewis responded, "Oh, hell! What you two need is a bullet between each of your eyes."

Bad Lewis went right on pushing the miners to continue the march, and hundreds more quickly joined. Some said they weren't sure whether to believe Keeney, or whether he was just saying what he'd been forced to say by General Bandholtz.

For their part, Keeney and Mooney suspected that Bad Lewis was secretly on Sheriff Don Chafin's payroll, an agent provocateur, getting the miners worked up only to have them walk into a carefully laid trap when they met Chafin's forces holding the high ground in fortified defensive positions all up and down the ridges of Blair Mountain.

When notice got back to Logan County that the miners might once again be coming, despite Bandholtz's and Keeney's and Mooney's best efforts, Chafin wasted no time ordering a thousand of his men up the mountain with their machine guns where they sat through the night, waiting for the Redneck Army to mount an attack.

Perhaps things might have turned out differently if the special trains promised by the governor had been sent to take the miners home. But that didn't happen—not until it was way too late. And perhaps things might have still turned out differently if Don Chafin hadn't decided, in the midst of everything, to send a posse over the mountain and down into Clothier to arrest the miners who had roughed up his deputies, taken their car, and forced them to hike back to Logan two weeks before.

Chafin's revenge squad—with nearly three hundred well-armed deputies and state police, it was more the size of a full-scale military company—set out from the town of Logan on Saturday, August 27. They were led by state police captain James Brockus, who'd had experience with this sort of thing when he served in the US Army in the Philippines in the early 1900s, helping crush a nationalist insurrection there. When they arrived in Clothier, they quickly tracked down and arrested eight of the miners supposedly responsible for that earlier humiliation, then forced them to march down the dirt road as human shields toward the town of Sharples where Brockus figured to make some more arrests.

If Brockus hadn't figured on running into a line of armed miners blocking the road, he probably should have, because that was who the group encountered just as they reached Sharples.

"Who are you?" Brockus shouted.

"By God that is our business," one of the miners answered.

Another miner demanded to know why they had come to Sharples.

Before Brockus could answer, one of his men yelled out: "We've come after you [expletive] miners!"

And with that, the night erupted. Three of the captured men went down immediately in a hail of bullets as both sides opened fire, the miners in the road joined by dozens of others hiding on porches, behind trees, and in nearby houses. It was impossible to know which side had shot the three captives, two of whom died.

The miners flooded Sharples with lights from their houses and from the nearby mine, all the better to spot their targets, sending Brockus and his men diving for cover in a ravine just off the road. Miraculously, no one in Brockus's company was killed or even wounded, and no other miners were hit, though the shooting went on for a while seemingly at point-blank range.

The other captives took advantage of the confusion and ran

off to safety, though the deputies quickly grabbed five more hostages, dragging them along as they made their careful retreat out of what was clearly a union stronghold. Brockus's men had no way of knowing that, in fact, they outnumbered the miners by probably ten to one, and most of the thousands of miners on the march toward Blair Mountain were still at least thirty miles away.

All night, Brockus led his men scrambling up the mountain in a circuitous route to safety. Once they got back to Logan, they discovered that they were short four deputies who had lost their way—wandering in the night and eventually captured back on Blair Mountain by a stealth unit of thirty miners.

Not long after the dust settled, the miners offered the deputies up for exchange in a prisoner swap. But the swap never happened.

News of the gun battle—what was already being called the "Sharples Massacre"—spread like wildfire up the Spruce Fork River back to the miners' encampment in Madison, morphing by the time it got there into a horror story of women and children, dozens of them, gunned down in cold blood by Chafin's minions.

No matter what anybody said—not Frank Keeney, not Governor Morgan, not General Bandholtz, not Mother Jones, not President Warren Harding himself—there was no turning back now.

CHAPTER SIXTEEN

"Time to lay down my Bible and pick up my rifle"

The trains in southern West Virginia quit running to anybody's notion of a schedule. Now they were all "Miners Specials"—flatcars and boxcars pulled by coal-powered engines commandeered throughout the Kanawha and New River coalfields, hauling militant miners in by the hundreds, closer and closer to what would soon be the combat zone. For thousands of others, the foot-march to Logan County continued, while hundreds more rode in cars and trucks (many of them hijacked at gunpoint). Some even rode into battle on horses and mules. One union observer said Sharples and Blair, the small mining towns at the base of Blair Mountain, were like Belgium on the eve of the war, "a monster powder keg awaiting only the smallest of sparks to launch one of the bloodiest industrial wars in the history of the world."

Newspapers around the country ran reports that bordered

Freight train loaded with armed miners makes its way through Boone County, West Virginia.

on hysteria, one even going so far as to call the entire state of West Virginia a "national stench and disgrace." On Monday, August 29, and again the next day, Governor Morgan sent telegrams to Washington begging the secretary of war to send in federal troops before everything exploded: "Danger of attack on Logan County by armed insurrections is so imminent that legislature cannot be assembled in time to eliminate probability of chaos and bloodshed."

Don Chafin decided to turn over command of his Logan Defenders—now 2,800 strong—to a colonel in the newly formed though undermanned National Guard, a war veteran named William Eubanks. Eubanks responded to the appointment by drinking heavily once he got to Logan and by all accounts keeping it up for most of the following week.

For a variety of reasons, not least of which was distrust of the

West Virginia politicians, President Harding was still reluctant to get involved. But with pressure mounting, he finally ordered the miners to stand down, using the overly formal language for which he'd become known.

"Whereas the Governor of West Virginia has represented that domestic violence exists in said State which the authorities of said State are unable to suppress," the edict began, "and, whereas it is provided in the Constitution of the United States that the United States shall protect each State. . . ."

The order went on like that for quite a while, pages of preamble, before finally concluding, "Therefore, I, Warren G. Harding, President of the United States, do hereby make proclamation and I do hereby command all persons engaged in said insurrection to disperse

The president's proclamation was printed in *The West Virginian* on September 1, 1921, just above a statement about Bandholtz's return to West Virginia and a report that Keeney and Mooney could not be found.

and retire peaceably to their respective abodes on or before 12 o'clock, noon, of the first day of September, 1921, and hereafter abandon said combinations and submit themselves to the laws and constituted authorities of said State."

General Bandholtz, who had just gotten back to Washington, unaware of the Sharples Massacre and thinking all was calm, was sent immediately back to West Virginia to make sure the miners complied. And in case they didn't, he was authorized to summon three army regiments that would be standing by, one in Ohio, one in Kentucky, and one in New Jersey, all close enough to reach West Virginia in a matter of hours.

A deeply frustrated Bandholtz pulled no punches in his after-action report, placing blame for the mess squarely on the governor and Don Chafin. "It is believed that the withdrawal of the invaders as promised by Keeney and Mooney would have been satisfactorily accomplished but for the tardy sending of trains," he wrote, "and particularly but for the ill-advised and ill-timed advance movement of the State constabulary on the night of August 27, resulting in bloodshed."

Not that it mattered anymore who was at fault. Two days later, when Chafin's biplanes flew over the thousands of miners massed at the base of Blair Mountain to drop fliers containing the president's proclamation, most didn't even bother to pick them up and read them.

The first unit up the mountain consisted of seventy miners, white and Black, led by Reverend John Wilburn, a part-time pastor/part-time miner from the town of Blair. Among the group, snaking through the thick underbrush to climb as close as they could to Chafin's defenses, were two of Wilburn's adult sons.

"Come on boys," he told the men. "We will eat dinner in Logan tomorrow." In a more pensive moment, he added, "The time has come for me to lay down my Bible and pick up my rifle and fight for my rights."

By some accounts, Wilburn and his followers set out on their own initiative. By other accounts, the generalissimo, Bill Blizzard, sent them and another party on scouting missions. Whichever was the case, by nightfall on August 30, 1921, Wilburn's company made it to the top of the ridge, a good mile and a half on a winding route up the mountain, where they slept out under the stars. As it happened, coming up the other side of Blair Mountain early the next morning in a Model T Ford, keeping to a narrow road, was one of Chafin's chief deputies, John Gore, along with two underlings. After a break to fix a flat tire—and to fortify themselves with a few belts of moonshine—they set back on their way, only to stop again, dead in their tracks, when they heard gunfire.

Nobody found out, then or later, who had been doing the shooting or where, but Reverend Wilburn and his company heard the gunshots as well. They headed in the direction they thought it was coming from—and straight into an encounter with Gore and his men.

The two parties froze on the open road, guns at the ready, but uncertain about pulling their triggers. It wasn't immediately clear to either side if the others were friend or foe.

So Reverend Wilburn demanded Gore and his men give the password.

What Gore should have said was "I come creeping." What he said instead was "Amen," and that was the end of them. The miners opened fire from six feet away, and all three deputies went down, their bodies riddled with bullets. Gore and the second victim were most likely dead before they landed. The third, seriously wounded, clung to life until Wilburn walked over, aimed his rifle at the deputy's forehead, and pulled the trigger.

One of the miners had also been shot in the exchange. The others began to carry him back down the mountain to Blair, but he died on the way. Besides the accidental shooting of a state trooper in Logan the day before, the four who died in the shootout—one miner and three deputies—were the first known casualties of the Battle of Blair Mountain.

Since Frank Keeney and Fred Mooney weren't anywhere around—hunkered down once again back in Charleston—it continued to fall onto the young Bill Blizzard to take charge of the miners' army, or as much "charge" as was possible given the unorganized nature of the insurrection. Blizzard was already a veteran of the guerilla mine wars dating back to 1912 and 1913, when his father was blacklisted for union activity and his mother had joined other union wives in tearing up train tracks in the middle of the night in support of the strikers.

After Reverend Wilburn's foray up the mountain, and those first casualties, Blizzard did his best to get his forces to regroup and redeploy. Everybody knew a frontal assault would be suicide on Blair Mountain, where the Logan Defenders had already had days to dig in, build up their breastworks, and otherwise prepare the mountain gaps against the invasion.

The strategy Blizzard and his advisers came up with instead, ordered and launched on the afternoon of August 31, was a pincer movement. Keeping some of his troops in reserve in Blair and Sharples, Blizzard sent half the attackers left and half to the right so they could come at Chafin's dug-in militia up on Blair Mountain from two sides at once. In the classic pincer movement, the two units would manage to also get behind the defenders, ultimately encircling them—cutting off supply lines and any avenue of retreat.

But the miners faced an uphill battle from the start—literally and figuratively. First, there was the steep grade of the mountains and the thick forest cover. It was a hard scramble just to climb into position—let alone to do so with weapons. Poor communication and difficulty coordinating so many union locals made things tougher still for the Redneck Army.

The biggest challenge of all, of course, even if the miners had operated all together in the pincer movement as a well-oiled war machine, was the cold, hard fact that Chafin's men held that high ground, an enormous advantage in every battle fought in just about every war ever. Not only did the defenders have the upper hand with their breastwork fortifications and machine-gun nests and lookouts and seemingly endless supply of ammunition, but also with the mountain gaps so thoroughly blocked by the Logan army—at the saddle of Blair Mountain, a mile or so north of there up Beech Creek, and even farther north at Crooked Creek Gap—there was no other path for the miners to take to cross into Logan and continue their march down to Mingo.

Still, undaunted, the miners crawled on their bellies up the mountain, crouching behind rocks and trees, hiding in the bushes. They hauled up behind them what few heavy guns they possessed, whether stolen or "liberated," as they sometimes said. A Gatling gun. A few Thompson submachine guns. Those lucky enough to lay their hands on tommy guns could fire off nine hundred rounds per minute from fifty- or one-hundred-round drum magazines. Mostly the miners carried whatever they had from back at home. Some had muzzle-loaded squirrel rifles. Some had old lever-action Model 1873 Winchester rifles from their service in Europe, or the cheaper surplus twelve-round Swiss Vetterli bolt-action rifles that flooded the market after the war.

When it came to ammunition and weapons, Chafin's men had more than their share. They used their superior rifles, tommy guns, and tripod-mounted machine guns to keep the miners pinned down hour after bloody scorching hour on that first, broiling ninety-degree day of the Battle of Blair Mountain.

The miners had greater numbers—10,000 to Don Chafin's 2,800—but the Logan army had a direct and much shorter supply line up from the town of Logan, with ammo and food and replacement troops and medical tents and dedicated headquarters in the swankiest hotel in town. They had direct lines of sight down on the invaders—and direct lines of fire. Chafin also had three biplanes that soon took to the air not only to shower the miners with those thousands of fliers with President Harding's proclamation, but also to drop tear gas and pipe bombs on the miners' camps. None of those, as it turned out, did any real damage. Several were duds. Others missed their mark. All were just a sideshow to the very real torrents of bullets that flew back and forth between the Redneck Army and the Logan Defenders.

The miners tried everything they could that first day of

fighting, including climbing trees once they got near enough to the heavy fortifications to get a decent shot. But Chafin's men spotted them there, too, and snipers brought several down. Every time one of the miners' units made a charge, they were driven back by the Logan army's overwhelming firepower. The most they could do was stuff cotton in their ears to keep from going deaf from the nonstop shooting.

CHAPTER SEVENTEEN

"Actual war is raging in Logan"

The closest the miners came to breaking through on that first day was their advance a few miles north of Blair, at Crooked Creek Gap, where Chafin's army had 1,200 defenders dug in. The group included various volunteer units led by various officials, but all were unofficially led by a notorious Baldwin-Felts agent named Antoine August "Tough Tony" Gaujot. Gaujot, though a Medal of Honor winner for heroic action in the Philippines during the Spanish-American War, was better known throughout coal country for his brutal treatment of miners during the 1912–1913 Paint Creek–Cabin Creek strike. He later served in WWI and rose to the rank of lieutenant colonel before returning to West Virginia and bolstering his "Tough Tony" nickname as a take-no-prisoners union-buster with Baldwin-Felts. Now at Crooked Creek Gap on the afternoon of August 31, he was back at it, manning a tripod machine gun that he didn't stop firing for hours until it literally melted down and jammed.

State police and mine guards in trenches on Blair Mountain.

A group of eighty miners from Cabin Creek were the first to run into the relentless machine-gun fire. The casualties mounted quickly. "Two boys was killed," the president of the Cabin Creek union chapter later recalled—a full fifty years after the battle. "Both were just out of the service and had on their uniforms. They thought they'd go up around a machine gun and capture the gunner. Evidently they got in his sights. . . . Because both of them were killed. One boy was hit six or seven times."

Gaujot and his men kept the miners pinned down for much of the afternoon, the torrent of bullets shredding the ground cover and blasting bare the trees. Veterans on both sides said it reminded them of the relentless battle with the Germans in the thick Argonne Forest.

Once Tough Tony's machine gun jammed, though—after three solid hours of firing—the miners seized their opportunity: they surged up the mountain, dragging their own Gatling gun along with them for a flank attack on Gaujot's position. Suddenly outgunned and outnumbered, the defenders were forced into a hurried retreat half a mile toward Logan.

When word got back to town, Don Chafin, or maybe it was the drunk but still somewhat effective Colonel Eubanks, sent a caravan of Model Ts racing up the mountain with more men and guns and ammo, setting up a second line of defense just two miles above the town.

One of the men sent up from Logan to defend Crooked Creek Gap in this second wave was none other than Isaac Brewer, who had stood side by side with Sid Hatfield and the miners in the Matewan shootout a year earlier, before turning on them in the trial in exchange for a $1,000 bribe.

Fortunately for the Home Guard—unfortunately for the miners—their second line held as the sun set on the first day of fighting.

Not that it calmed the nervous citizens down below. "ACTUAL WAR IS RAGING IN LOGAN," screamed one local headline. *The Reds were coming! The Bolsheviks were hammering at the door!* The president of the Logan Coal Operators Association sent a desperate telegram to a West Virginia congressman: "Unless troops sent by midnight tonight the Town of Logan will be attacked by an army of from four to eight thousand

Reds and great loss of life and property sustained." The congressman shot off a message in turn to the White House, telling President Harding his proclamation had come to naught.

Emergency meetings were called. Nervous hands were wrung. Lights were kept on all night in both capitals—Charleston and Washington. The wheels of government started to turn.

Meanwhile, nightfall did little to quell the fighting, as reconnaissance patrols stumbled into one another in the dark, and flashes of gunfire lit up the mountains. "Someone spies the dark shadow of an armed man stealing along the road and lets go at it," said one defender. "Immediately the whole face of the two mountainsides spit forth angry protesting tongues of flame from which bullets whistle and ricochet down the road. The miners returned the fire—the report of the first rifle shot hardly begins to echo before the pinkish mushroom of flame and the following crack of a revolver or rifle tell the tale."

Frank Keeney and Fred Mooney, the leaders and brain trust of UMWA District 17, were nowhere near the front lines that first day of fighting. And by the second day, September 1, they weren't even in West Virginia. Several union men showed up at Mooney's home in Charleston the night of August 31, messengers from the front, sent to let him know that the Redneck Army had launched the first salvo in the attack—and the second and the third and more besides. The war on Don Chafin and Logan County and martial law in Mingo was happening, the visitors said, whether Keeney and Mooney were behind it or not.

That was how Fred Mooney remembered it, anyway, years

later. At the time, plenty of others maintained that though Keeney and Mooney were never present on the battlefront, they nonetheless were still directing at least some of the action from behind the scenes—even all the way across the state line in Ohio.

Early the next morning, the two men traveled to a union safe house in Columbus, Ohio—not to avoid taking command of the Battle of Blair Mountain, but to steer clear of arrest. Because they'd also just received notice that a Mingo County grand jury had indicted them for several crimes, including murder, from the Three Days' Battle a year ago. And not only that, but they might soon be facing charges in Logan County as well for the deaths of the three deputies, including Don Chafin's right-hand man John Gore, killed by Reverend Wilburn and his men.

After the murders of Sid Hatfield and Ed Chambers in McDowell County, Keeney and Mooney were under no illusion that they could expect a fair trial in either case. Their best bet was to stay out of handcuffs altogether, and to do that, they had to stay out of West Virginia.

Back on Blair Mountain, Day Two of the fighting was more of the same: The miners clawing their way up to the mountain passes, holding close to whatever cover they could, whatever trees and scrub hadn't yet been obliterated by the fierce and seemingly nonstop fusillades raining down on them from the Logan Defenders. Flank attacks that kept failing. Sniper fire that only sometimes found its mark. Machine gun vs. machine gun. Suffering and dying in the brutal heat.

Day Two was when Don Chafin had his biplanes outfitted

with homemade bombs—six-inch pipes crammed full of black powder and nuts and bolts. The closest any came to hitting its mark was one that blew a crater in the ground next to a school that had been converted into a makeshift hospital. The miners returned fire with their rifles, chasing off the errant bombers, but kept an anxious watch on the skies from then on.

It was a long, hard day. The fighting went back and forth, with thousands and thousands of bullets fired, but the miners could barely hold their positions, let alone make any discernible progress.

That second evening, Don Chafin told reporters that thirty

One of Don Chafin's planes crashed into a house in Logan County. Fortunately, no one was killed.

miners had been killed, but only three of his men. Others put the death total at more than two hundred. There were reports of the miners' army spiriting away the bodies of fifty men for secret burials in family plots back home. All anyone could say for certain was that the death toll among the miners was much greater than it was for the Logan Defenders.

While all this was going on, General Bandholtz, back in Charleston on orders from the president, was running his own reconnaissance, sending his aides out into the field on scouting missions to assess whether there was any chance that the miners would voluntarily stand down once again.

The answer he got back wasn't just no, but it was a resounding "Hell no!"—even after Bandholtz's men guaranteed the miners safe passage back to their homes if they'd only agree to quit the fight.

Bandholtz was still furious at the governor and Chafin for provoking the insurrection days earlier, just when he had managed to negotiate a truce. But now, the time was past for worrying about who was to blame and why. The way Bandholtz saw it, the straight truth of the matter was a civil war was raging in West Virginia, and it had to be stopped. So the following day, September 2, he made the call to Washington, the White House, and the secretary of war: send in the troops.

CHAPTER EIGHTEEN

"It'll take the miners a week to bury the dead"

The order went out that same day, Friday, September 2, for those 2,100 soldiers standing ready in three nearby army bases to deploy to southern West Virginia. Troop trains pulled out from New Jersey, Ohio, and Kentucky, hauling what were described by some news accounts as elite infantry units and by others as mostly green recruits. Whichever it was, they were well armed and well supplied and en route to the hinterlands to put down the miners' rebellion and restore peace and order, such as it could be or had ever been. For good measure, the secretary of war ordered a chemical warfare unit to ship out to West Virginia from an armory in Maryland with a load of 150-pound tear-gas bombs, while a heavy squadron of twenty-one US Army Air Service de Havilland fighter-bombers and Martin bombers were sent to Charleston in case they were needed—though through a series of mishaps, crashes, and mechanical failures, only fourteen actually made it there.

West Virginia: The Same Old Line-up

"The Same Old Line up": cartoon shows a soldier with a rifle trained on a West Virginia mine worker. Behind him are President Warren Harding and a mine owner.

The miners didn't know the troops were coming. Not right away. And not before they launched a double offensive, one yet again on Blair Gap, and the other, the next day, against Tough Tony Gaujot and his men on Crooked Creek. On Blair, the miners first sent a secret patrol over the mountain to blow up a railroad bridge on the Logan side to prevent reinforcements from coming in. Although one of the Defenders discovered the dynamite before it detonated, the miners pressed ahead with their plan. They faked a frontal assault, a feint, to draw enemy fire, then attacked on both flanks and nearly forced Chafin's men out of their mountain fortress. But the return fire—according to one account, a hundred Logan army bullets to every one the miners managed to get off—proved too much in the end. And in the midst of all this, word did finally filter down the line that federal troops were on the way to Blair, dashing the miners' hopes and their commitment.

It was one thing to take on Don Chafin and his militia. But insurrection against the US government? War against the very army in which so many of them had once served? Not a chance.

"The idea, in fact, was totally unthinkable to them," author Lon Savage explained. "Their enemy was nearer home: the coal operator; the deputy sheriff hired by the operator to enforce the law the way the operator liked the law enforced; and above all, the private Baldwin-Felts detectives and others collectively known as 'thugs,' who, protected by the operator-paid deputies,

Federal troops arrived by train with extensive supplies.

US Army tents at Blair Mountain.

broke both the laws of man and the principles of morality that others adhered to, by spying, by bullying, by violence, by gun."

In the days that followed, trains pulling flatcars crammed with US Army soldiers snaked their way into West Virginia at twenty miles an hour through hills and hollows, hauling cannons and wagons and horses and boxes upon boxes of ammunition and other supplies until they arrived at both sides of Blair Mountain.

When they got there, not a single, solitary miner raised a weapon against them.

Newspaper headlines just the day before had shouted about the latest developments on the battlefield: "PLANES DROP BOMBS OF TNT ON MINERS," "HARD BATTLE ON TWO FRONTS OF LOGAN COUNTY LINE." But as soon as the troops arrived and the fighting stopped, they turned their focus to the aftermath: "MANY DEATHS AMONG MINERS REPORTED," "IT'LL TAKE THE MINERS A WEEK TO BURY THE DEAD."

When the first federal troop train reached Madison, the original staging area for the miners' march, they encountered Bill Blizzard almost right off the bat, shuffling up in a badly wrinkled suit and soiled shirt and tie. A *New York Times* reporter recorded the exchange between Blizzard and the army captain who interrogated him.

"Are you the general of the miners' army?" Blizzard was asked.

"What army?" he responded, then added, "I guess the boys'll listen to me all right."

An obviously weary Blizzard offered to go up the miners' line to call off the fighting and convince them to return to their homes. "I can get all our fellows out of the hills by daylight," he said.

Before the captain agreed to let him go, he ordered his men to search Blizzard for weapons. They found a loaded pistol but returned it as soon as Blizzard produced a legal permit to carry.

"Does this mean you are going to allow only men with permits to keep their guns?" Blizzard asked, worried about what would happen if the miners gave up their guns while Chafin's men were allowed to keep theirs. He protested, "Our boys'll be unarmed and those Baldwin-Felts thugs will just shoot 'em down whenever they please."

The army wouldn't budge on the issue of permits, so Blizzard excused himself and spent the next several hours spreading the word to as many of the miners as he could find: *The*

*war's over. The army's going to confiscate your guns, so hide 'em
or lose 'em.*

When Blizzard returned to Madison, streams of retreating
miners soon followed, surrendering at checkpoints to the otherwise idle troops. Several hundred weapons were confiscated.
Thousands more were left hidden on the hills and mountains,
buried on farms and in fields.

Three miners surrendering their weapons to waiting federal soldiers.

"That's why you don't see the guns," Blizzard said. "When we need 'em again, we'll know where to look for 'em."

Although many miners got rid of their unpermitted firearms in other, more creative ways, the federal troops at checkpoints amassed a large collection of weapons.

Meanwhile, on the other side of the mountain, what army officials found was largely a state of drunken chaos, leaving many to wonder how the Logan Defenders had managed to hold the mountain gaps for as long as they did.

One army officer, upon reaching the hotel headquarters of Colonel Eubanks, the commander of Chafin's militia, determined that Eubanks and his staff were "so unmistakably under the influence of liquor as to render them unfit in our opinion for an orderly transition of business." Another officer, after a general inspection of the situation in Logan, concluded "that there had been dissension among the leaders, lack of a carefully organized plan of defense, and that the state of intoxication found upon our arrival had endured for at least most of the preceding twenty-four hours."

So perhaps it wasn't so preposterous that among the miners, now making their tired way back to their homes all up and down the Kanawha Valley and across West Virginia, many held to the belief that if the US Army hadn't been ordered in by the president, the Redneck Army would have ultimately prevailed.

Even at that, many of the miners were convinced they'd won the war, despite the impasse in the Battle of Blair Mountain—because surely the federal troops, and the intervention of the government, would set things right in Medieval West Virginia. Freedom of speech. Due process under the law. The right of free association. An end to the tyranny and oppression of the coal operators and corrupt sheriffs like Don Chafin. These weren't Bolshevik ideas. They were bedrock American values. And it was high time somebody—the US Army would do just fine—stepped in and ensured the miners and their families got to have them. And an end to martial law in Mingo County while they were at it.

But Governor Morgan wasn't ready to give up all that easily, and neither were the coal operators, all of whom implored the government to hold the miners accountable and bring charges against the whole lot of them, especially the District 17 UMWA leaders. The owners and operators once again lambasted the supposed "outside agitators"—Reds and Socialists who'd come into West Virginia to foment a workers' revolution, in defiance of what they joined the business class nationwide in calling "the American Way."

For their part, General Bandholtz and President Harding just wanted to move on. Any labor conflict still going on in West Virginia would have to be handled by West Virginians themselves, and when the trains left the southern counties, days after the end of the hostilities, all 2,100 brown-uniformed US Army soldiers were on board, waving so long to the Mountain State.

That left it to Morgan, the operators, and the politicians to make the next move. If the federal government didn't want to deal with the insurrection any further, well, then the state would have to step up and do the job themselves.

The miners barely had time to settle back into their homes before state police and deputy sheriffs swept through the mining towns and tent cities making arrests. County jails were soon full to overflowing as 550 miners and union officials were hit with a thousand charges ranging from murder to treason and everything in between.

No more shots were fired, but the labor war in West Virginia was far from over. The battle was about to shift from the killing fields back to the courthouse. And not just any courthouse, but one of the most historic in America—the very courthouse where sixty years earlier the abolitionist John Brown was sentenced to hang for treason, and where now Generalissimo Bill Blizzard would be the first of the miners to stand trial on the same capital charge.

CHAPTER NINETEEN

"We was all just leaders, in a manner of speaking"

The number often cited—there are some discrepancies—is 985. That's how many indictments came out of Logan and Mingo Counties following the Battle of Blair Mountain, only some of which, including Bill Blizzard's treason trial, were held at the Jefferson County Courthouse in Charles Town, West Virginia, 250 miles to the north and far enough away from coal country that both sides could be at least somewhat confident of finding an impartial jury.

The deck seemed stacked otherwise against Blizzard and the rest of those charged, including Frank Keeney and Fred Mooney, who'd negotiated their surrender directly to the governor because they feared assassination if they were to turn themselves in to any of the southern counties. They spent time behind bars in Charleston awaiting trial but were shipped down to Logan at one point anyway, where they also sat for a couple of months in Don Chafin's jail before facing—and being exonerated for—all the various and sundry charges there and back in Mingo. But that all came later.

United Mine Workers leaders and lawyers at the Jefferson County Courthouse for the treason trials.

Meanwhile, at the Jefferson County Courthouse, the coal operators let it be known that they were paying for the prosecution of the mine leaders. And not only that, but when the Jefferson County prosecutor refused to take on the treason cases against the miners, the coal operators association's chief legal counsel gave himself the job.

Most newspapers covering the trials viewed the case for

treason skeptically. "We see no reason for charging these workers with any such offense," wrote one Maryland paper. "On the
face of it the charge looks like a libel on them and a slander."

The *New York Times*, usually a reliably conservative,
pro-business voice in these matters, denounced the treason
charges in even stronger terms. "Whatever their offenses, the
union miners and their leaders were not trying to subvert the
Government of West Virginia in whole or in part. . . . In West Virginia indictments for treason seem to be thrown about as care-
lessly as if they were indictments for the larceny of a chicken."

The coal operators obviously saw things in a different light.
The *Williamson, W.V. Daily News*, coal-owned and operated,
declared the union leaders guilty even before the trials were
scheduled.

"These men aided, abetted, and encouraged insurrectionists
in their mad march from the heart of Kanawha County to the
edge of Logan," the *Daily News* wrote, "and each is liable to
indictment for murder and larceny, if not treason. . . . The juries
of Logan and Boone Counties have the opportunity to send them
to the penitentiary or to the gallows."

Blizzard's trial took the good part of four weeks, with testimony going back and forth—some from miners who had
turned on him, much more of it from those who remained
loyal—about the degree to which Blizzard may have been in
charge, or if he was even present at the foot of Blair Mountain
during the conflict.

Years later, one of the miners who'd taken part in the insurrection reflected: "A lot of people will tell you that Bill Blizzard
was the leader of it all. Now Bill's one of the finest people who

ever lived, don't get me wrong. . . . But he wasn't the leader any more than the rest of us was, from the way I see it. We was all just leaders, in a manner of speaking."

The handwriting was on the wall in Blizzard's trial when the judge gave his narrow interpretation of the West Virginia treason statute, saying that treason required the defendant to wage war against the *state*, which had never been the case with the Redneck Army. They were loyal West Virginians, after all. Loyal Americans. Their fight was against the coal operators and their hired thugs. That was who they were going after up on Blair Mountain. And it had been a peaceful march, they argued, until Don Chafin sent Captain Brockus and the state police and those Logan County deputies over to Sharples where they attacked innocent miners and their families.

The union leaders were so sure of acquittal that when they met up on a ballfield one Sunday afternoon during the trial, they made light of the situation with a lineup card listing the

The mine workers took a break during the treason trials for a little baseball.

players by name, position, charge, and amount of bail: "William Blizzard, right field, treason, murder, etc., $33,000."

Blizzard's next trial, for murder, didn't go any better than the first—at least not for the prosecution—and once he was acquitted and other charges against him were dropped, supporters carried the UMWA District 17 vice president triumphantly through the streets of Charles Town.

The coal operators were able to score a few convictions, most notably the murder charges against Reverend John Wilburn and one of his sons, who were sentenced to eleven years in prison. They also managed to convince a jury to convict a low-level union official named Walter Allen of treason. But that was pretty much where things ended. James M. Cain, a *Baltimore Sun* reporter who would later become an acclaimed novelist, was disgusted by the verdict.

"By a jury of his peers," Cain wrote, "packed against him and bearing instructions virtually proclaiming his guilt; on the flimsiest sort of evidence and with not the ghost of a chance at a fair trial from start to finish, Walter Allen, union miner, has been solemnly adjudged to be a traitor to that section of coal operators' real estate known as the sovereign State of West Virginia."

Most of the charges against the miners were eventually dismissed, or thrown out, or indefinitely postponed. Those that did go to trial, like the cases against Frank Keeney and Fred Mooney, mostly ended in acquittals or hung juries, some in Charles Town, others back in the southern counties. After Walter Allen was convicted, he was released pending an appeal, but he never showed back up for court. Instead, he skipped out on bail and was never seen or heard from again.

The Wilburns served three years in prison until Mother Jones, in her last act on behalf of the miners of West Virginia, convinced the governor to commute the remaining eight years of their sentences.

In the US Senate, the Kenyon Committee Hearings resumed, briefly, a few months after the Battle of Blair Mountain, with heart-wrenching testimony from Jessie Hatfield and Sallie Chambers about the murders of their husbands on the steps to the McDowell County Courthouse. Union officials provided evidence that U.S. Steel, one of the most powerful corporations in America, had extensive interests in the coal-mining operations of West Virginia and pulled many of the political strings in the state—to the detriment of the miners. Senator Kenyon himself made two investigative trips to the Mountain State and compiled additional evidence of the mistreatment of mine workers and their families.

But in the end, all that came of it was a wordy report lamenting the harsh working and living conditions for the miners in West Virginia and decrying the corporate roots of the conflict there. All talk, in other words, but no action.

Perhaps the most pressing concern for the miners, who kept up their strike in Mingo County for a full year after Blair Mountain, was that the seemingly endless trials, along with the ongoing cost of the strike, ended up bankrupting the District 17 coffers. Frank Keeney and Fred Mooney were eventually forced out of their leadership positions. But the mining industry faced problems far beyond Mingo County as well. The demand for coal, already falling after the end of the war in Europe, went over a cliff in the years that followed as the economy turned more and more to oil and natural gas. Jobs dried up. The weakened union was forced to accept pay cuts even in the unionized mines to the north. Union membership went into a nosedive.

And in the aftermath of the Battle of Blair Mountain, few outside coal country seemed to care. To the rest of America, at least those who took their cues from the newspaper headlines, the mine workers were just a bunch of Socialist hillbillies anyway. And dangerous ones at that.

And the coal operators did their best to reinforce this message in West Virginia. They brought the then famous evangelist Billy Sunday, known as much for his blowtorch conservatism as for his fire-and-brimstone sermons, to speak in Charleston. At an outdoor revival attended by thousands, he denounced the union and its leaders in no uncertain terms.

"I'd rather be in hell with Cleopatra, John Wilkes Booth and Charles Guiteau than live on earth with such human lice," he

The notorious evangelist Billy Sunday said he'd rather be in hell "with Cleopatra, John Wilkes Booth and Charles Guiteau" than live on earth with the union miners of West Virginia.

preached, for some reason equating the queen of the Nile with the two presidential assassins. "If I were the Lord for about fifteen minutes, I'd smack the bunch so hard that there would be nothing left for the devil to levy on but a bunch of whiskers and a bad smell."

Meanwhile, over the next ten years, as the nation went into an economic slide that turned into the Great Depression, things got worse and worse for the workers Billy Sunday had branded as "human lice," and especially for their children. In 1923, the average miner earned $853 a year. Six years later, it was down to $588. In 1933, as the Depression ground through a fourth year, those few who still held on to their mining jobs made a paltry $235.

The journalist Lorena Hickok, after witnessing the ensuing poverty firsthand, inspired her close friend, First Lady Eleanor Roosevelt, to visit and lobby for impoverished West Virginia after Franklin Roosevelt was elected president in 1932. No one, it seemed, had been hit harder by the Depression than the mine families.

"Scott's run, a coal-mining community, not far from Morgantown, was the worst place I'd even seen," wrote Hickok. "In a gutter, along the main street through the town, there was stagnant, filthy water, which the inhabitants used for drinking, cooking, washing, and everything else imaginable. On either side of the street were ramshackle houses, black with coal dust, which most Americans would not have considered fit for pigs. And in those houses every night children went to sleep hungry, on piles of bug-infested rags, spread out on the floor. There were rats in those houses.

First Lady Eleanor Roosevelt, concerned about the poverty and harsh living conditions for mine families, tours one of the mines in a coal car.

"As I proceeded through the state I found other places just as bad. Everywhere, grimy, undernourished, desperate people so hungry that they could not wait for the vegetables to mature in the pathetic little gardens they tried to raise on mountainsides so steep that they must have had to shoot the seeds in to make them stick. They would dig up the tiny potatoes long before they had reached their full size and pick the tomatoes and eat them while they were still green."

Of course, even before the economy tanked, such appalling conditions weren't uncommon in the coalfields of West Virginia. It was true that some miners—not very many, but some—were Socialists. But to the extent that they embraced any sort of ideology, it was that they ought to be able to earn enough to take care of their children.

"Employers want to measure wages in cold dollars and cents," Frank Keeney once said, "while the miners insist that they be measured in human values, not by what they will actually purchase of the necessities of life. The miners take the position that low wages deprive children of education, of good food, destroy self-respect, and drive men to degradation."

Which was why, in the face of the collapse of the union following the treason trials, the story didn't end. Frank Keeney never went away, not entirely, and not for long. And he never stopped organizing. Even when UMWA membership in West Virginia plummeted, dropping to fewer than a thousand by the end of the 1920s, the miners never gave up the fight for social and economic justice.

"Imagine 23,000 coal miners under the iron heel of the gunmen system for twenty years," wrote Fred Mooney in his autobiography, discovered and published years later. "Think of the crushed hopes, smothered ambitions, cracked heads, and the thousands of insults to which they had been subjected."

They may not have won the Battle of Blair Mountain, and the fight might have gone dormant for a while, but it wasn't in the DNA of the West Virginia miners to quit altogether—not then, not ever. No matter how long it took, no matter how many sacrifices had to be made, they were bound and determined that in the end they would still find a way to win the West Virginia coal mine war.

CHAPTER TWENTY

"Hallowed ground"

Frank Keeney, forced into exile from the union by the national president, John L. Lewis, returned in 1931 to start a West Virginia branch of the Reorganized United Mine Workers of America, a reform-minded breakaway from the UMWA. In two weeks' time, 20,000 men took the new union's oath of obligation, jump-starting a whole new generation of activist miners in the Mountain State. The initiative was short-lived, only lasting a couple of years, but during that brief span, Keeney and his followers organized multiple strikes, held mass marches on the capital, and kept the fight for unionization and miners' rights alive and kicking.

One year earlier, the workers of America had lost one of their leading figures with the passing of ninety-one-year-old Mother Jones, a major blow to the union cause. One of the last things she did was donate what little money she had to the Reorganized United Mine Workers. They didn't like the way things were going with John L. Lewis and the old UMWA and neither did she. In a final interview, she reflected on her life's work, saying, "I've done the best I could to make the world a better place for poor, hard-working people."

It was a fitting epitaph.

If she'd lived just a few years longer, Mother Jones would have been thrilled to see the changes that were just over the horizon.

The first was long-sought federal legislation, years in the making, outlawing yellow-dog contracts, which workers had been forced to sign if they wanted a job in the mines, and which said they could be fired if they ever joined a union. That legislation also ended the freewheeling use of court injunctions in labor disputes.

That new law alone set coal operators' heads spinning, especially in West Virginia where they'd long relied on both methods for stomping out union activity.

Then, in 1932, after Franklin Roosevelt took office, a newly energized Congress passed the National Industrial Recovery Act, which among other progressive actions finally, formally, and officially gave workers the legal right to join unions. It was a new day in the coalfields of West Virginia. A new day for workers everywhere in America.

"All the demons in hell can't keep us from organizing Logan County now," crowed one union miner.

With Prohibition laws in full effect, another obstacle to organizing in Logan disappeared when Sheriff Don Chafin was sentenced to two years in a federal penitentiary for running an illegal bootleg liquor operation.

In June 1933, there were only seventeen members of the UMWA left in West Virginia, most having long since resigned to keep their desperately needed jobs, or left the state to find work elsewhere, or joined Keeney's reform union for its brief run. But by the end of 1934, once the new law took effect, 70,000 West Virginia coal miners had taken the UMWA oath of obligation. That number rose to 100,000 four years later—a whopping 98 percent of the men working underground in the Mountain State, including virtually every single one in Bloody Mingo County.

In short order, the union was able to negotiate what became known as the Appalachian Agreement with the largest mine operators' association in the region, guaranteeing mine workers an eight-hour workday, a forty-hour workweek, and a base rate of pay in line with what miners were making in the union mines in other states. Not only that, but the owners agreed they would no longer require workers to accept company scrip for their pay or to shop in company stores. There'd be checkweighmen approved by the workers, a multistep grievance process for firing workers, and a simple check-off system to collect union dues. The operators also promised not to hire any boys younger than seventeen.

And most important of all, they agreed to end the mine guard system, sounding the death knell for the hated Baldwin-Felts Detective Agency.

Historian Lon Savage once called Mingo County "hallowed

ground." Filmmaker John Sayles, who made a critically acclaimed movie about the West Virginia mine wars in 1987, said the story was "as much a part of our heritage as that of the Alamo or Gettysburg or the winning of the West."

Why then, Savage wanted to know, had the story of the Matewan Massacre—and the mass insurrection that followed—been buried, hidden all this time from the schoolchildren of West Virginia and from the rest of America?

An aerial view of Matewan, West Virginia, today.

Historian David Corbin wondered much the same thing. "During a dozen years of public schooling in West Virginia, I never heard about the great West Virginia Mine Wars," he wrote. "Instead, I was taught happy and pleasant things about our state. This included such bits of information like the location of the world's largest clothespin factory and the world's biggest ashtray. . . . To be able to counter any disparaging remarks outsiders may have made about our state, my school friends and I learned about every West Virginian who ever achieved national prominence."

That list, according to Corbin, included a Nobel Prize novelist, Pearl S. Buck, along with a long-forgotten comedian named Soupy Sales and the goofy actor Don Knotts from the old black-and-white *Andy Griffith* TV show.

"When we were told of the importance West Virginia held in relation to the rest of the nation, we were not informed of the fact that our coal heated its homes, fueled its industries, and powered its battleships for decades," Corbin wrote. "Nor were we told about the thousands of West Virginians who died getting that coal out of the ground. We were not told of the struggle these people underwent for safer working conditions and a better standard of living; that is, the struggle for their union. No, nothing about that."

Frank Keeney's great-grandson, who grew up hearing stories about his great-grandfather, remembers being surprised, and deeply disappointed, when he studied West Virginia history in school, and later taught it, and there was *still* virtually nothing about the mine wars, or Frank Keeney, or the other important figures from the state's labor history in his textbooks.

Part of the answer was in the long-held, and undeniably negative, stereotypes of West Virginians, then and now—so who cared if they killed one another in the streets of Matewan, no matter what the reason? Sure, it made national headlines right after it happened, all the way to the *New York Times*, but only briefly. Then nothing out of West Virginia until the next spasm of violence. And it seemed to have always been that way—at least in the popular consciousness. In 2010, the History Channel made yet another TV series about the Hatfields and McCoys starring the actor Kevin Costner, the Appalachian feud story that never seems to die. For most of the past century, it has seemed as though everything that came out of West Virginia— just about the only thing—was the backwoods stereotype, the image of hidden mountain moonshine stills replaced over time by trailer park meth and fentanyl labs. Drugs and violence and poverty.

And it's all had an impact, not only on how America views West Virginia, but also on how West Virginians, and especially young West Virginians, view themselves. In a recent survey of young people growing up in Appalachia, 78 percent said that the negative stereotypes hurt the state's ability to attract business investments, and 64 percent said the stereotypes hurt their sense of self-esteem. More than half—the study called them "Leavers"—said they were planning to move out of West Virginia once they were done with school. Only a third, the "Stayers," thought they might stick around.

In such an environment, is it any wonder Matewan and the mine wars have been all but forgotten?

But there's more to the buried history than just the matter of the stereotypes. A lot more. And a lot more to the answer about why anyone today should care.

One of the principal reasons the story has been overlooked is that through much of the twentieth century, the powers that be in West Virginia, the coal owners and their politicians, ran a deliberate disinformation campaign, seeking to sell the rest of America, and the schoolchildren of West Virginia, on a series of myths—*lies*, really—about mining coal.

It started in March 1920, when 150 West Virginia business leaders, many of them coal executives and mine owners, gathered in the state capital. Their purpose was to figure out a way to rein in the out-of-control narrative that was painting such a sorry—though all-too-accurate—picture in the national press of deplorable living and working conditions in the coalfields: the feudal mine camps and company towns, the violent labor clashes, the brutal mine-guard system. Even one of their own, former governor William Glasscock, had expressed his disdain about the operators' use of the Baldwin-Felts agents as their private police force. "No man worthy of the name likes to be guarded by another armed with blackjacks, revolvers, and Winchester while earning his daily bread," an investigation he authorized way back in 1912 had concluded. "It is repugnant to the spirit of the laboring man and we believe the opinion of the American people."

By the end of that March 1920 meeting, the West Virginia business leaders had come up with a plan—not to improve conditions for miners, but to form a propaganda arm, primarily through funding for an organization they named the American Constitutional Association. Its announced purpose, according to then governor John Cornwell, was to promote "Americanism," which he defined as "respect for the constitutional authorities, obedience to the law and preservation of order." One way to do that, they decided, was to influence the selection of textbooks in the West Virginia schools, and what better way to accomplish *that* than to write one themselves?

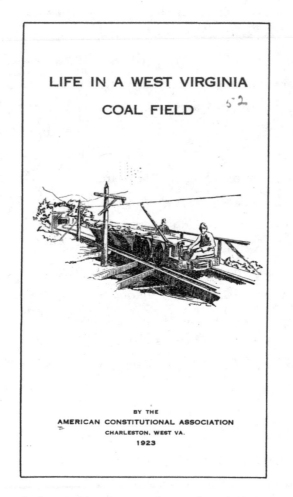

Book cover of the mine owners' rosy–and stunningly false–depiction of life for mine families in the West Virginia coalfields.

Which was exactly what they did, hiring an educator and publisher named Phil Conley to author a social studies textbook, *West Virginia: Yesterday and Today*, that soon went into classrooms throughout the state and stayed there for the next forty years, well into the 1970s, unchallenged. Nowhere in Conley's book, through eleven re-printings and "revisions," was there a single mention of Sid Hatfield, or the Baldwin-Felts mine guards, or the May 19, 1920, Battle of Matewan—or of what happened a year later, in 1921, when those 10,000 union miners, most of them wearing their work coveralls and red bandannas, took up their guns and fought a pitched battle against a heavily armed paramilitary force backed by the coal companies in the Battle of Blair Mountain. In fact, there was virtually no mention of the strikes, or the union, anywhere in the coal operators' version of West Virginia history.

Not content with his social studies text, Conley also wrote a sweet little children's book called *Life in a West Virginia Coal Field* that painted a rosy—and stunningly false—picture of the lives of miners and their families under the paternal care of the mine owners, who supposedly looked after their every need. And once again, in *Life in a West Virginia Coal Field* as in *West Virginia: Yesterday and Today*, there wasn't a single word about any Baldwin-Felts gun thugs, or criminally lax safety standards, or the mine disasters that had taken so many lives.

The mine owners' American Constitutional Association made sure Conley's children's book flooded the classrooms and libraries of West Virginia schools, where it, too, stayed for decades and can still be found on shelves today.

CHAPTER TWENTY-ONE

"Montani semper liberi"

They're all gone now—the heroes and villains of the West Virginia coal mine wars. Frank Keeney spent most of his adult life fighting for the union cause, a cause that eventually left him behind. From the UMWA, he joined the short-lived Reorganized UMWA, then the even shorter-lived West Virginia Mine Workers, finally ending up as an organizer for the Progressive Miners of America until it, too, folded. After that, he ran an orange juice stand, a grocery store, a wildcat oil drilling operation, a labor newspaper, and a nightclub in Charleston, West Virginia, that was eventually shut down for not having a proper liquor license. A working man to the end, Keeney worked one last job as a parking lot attendant in Charleston. He died in 1970 at eighty-eight.

Fred Mooney, whose first wife died when his children were small, eventually remarried. After his expulsion from the union, he moved around the country taking on various jobs, including working for a time as a coal mine supervisor. Frank Keeney recruited him to organize the northern part of West Virginia for Keeney's rogue West Virginia Mine Workers union that lasted just a few short years in the early 1930s. Mooney twice ran for state legislature in West Virginia and lost both times. One night in 1952, when he was at work, some dynamite that had been planted in his wife's bedroom exploded. His wife and children were home at the time but escaped serious injury. Police believed that Mooney had set the explosion, though it was never proven and never determined why. Mooney took his own life shortly after.

Bill Blizzard, the second-generation union man, stayed active as an officer in the UMWA for more than forty years, until 1955 when he had his own falling out with union president John L. Lewis. He left after getting into a fistfight with Lewis's brother and subsequently took up farming for what turned out to be his last three years until he died at sixty-five.

Tom Felts turned his back on West Virginia after the demise of the mine guard system. He followed his mentor William Baldwin into the banking business in southwest Virginia, was elected to two terms as a Virginia state senator, and shut down the Baldwin-Felts Detective Agency altogether in 1937, four months before his death. He was sixty-seven.

Don Chafin only served a few months of his two-year sentence for bootlegging, but he was finished as sheriff and would no longer wield the absolute control he had held for so long over Logan County. He eventually moved to Huntington, West Virginia, spent years as a lobbyist for the coal industry, and retired as one of the wealthiest men in the city, living in a penthouse he had built on top of one of Huntington's leading banks, which he also owned. He, too, was sixty-seven when he died in 1954—from a bad heart.

Several years after killing Sid Hatfield, Charles E. Lively, one of the more despicable characters in America's labor history, was charged with sexually assaulting a teenage girl. He managed to avoid prosecution; a codefendant went to prison. A few years after that, Lively was convicted of violently assaulting his wife and children—and shooting one of his sons. The son survived, and when Lively got out of prison, the son he had shot returned the favor, shooting and wounding his newly freed father. Lively also survived. After abandoning his family, Lively added bigamy to his growing list of offenses, marrying another woman while still married to his first wife, Icie. Late in life and in failing health, he left wife number two and returned to Icie, who inexplicably took him in. Lively, by that time nearly blind, took his own life in 1962, at his home in Huntington. The .38-caliber pistol found next to his body was the same gun he'd used during his years as a Baldwin-Felts agent and spy.

When Mother Jones died in 1930, 15,000 mourners showed up for the funeral in Mount Olive, Illinois—so many that they had to set up loudspeakers in the Catholic church so the massive crowd gathered outside could hear. Tens of thousands more listened in on a labor radio station out of Chicago and wept openly as Father John Maguire, Mother Jones's longtime friend and a labor activist in his own right, delivered the eulogy.

"My dear friends," he said, "today in gorgeous mahogany-furnished and carefully-guarded offices in distant capitals, wealthy mine owners and capitalists are breathing sighs of

Mother Jones near the end of her life

relief. Today upon the plains of Illinois, the hillsides and valleys of Pennsylvania and West Virginia, in California, Colorado and British Columbia, strong men and toil worn women are weeping tears of bitter grief. The reasons are the same. Mother Jones is dead."

Her hell-raising spirit, it should hardly need saying, still lives on in the hearts of working people—as well as in the pages of *Mother Jones* magazine, one of the nation's premier muck-raking publications that for the past fifty years has been a leading voice for progressive politics and workers' rights.

Matewan, West Virginia, tucked in a wide bend of the Tug River on the Kentucky border in southern West Virginia, looks much the same as it did that fateful day in 1920 when those dozen Baldwin-Felts men ran into Sid Hatfield and Cabell Testerman and their friends. The train station is still there. Sid and Jessie's old apartment has been kept as it was. Several buildings are still pocked with bullet holes from the shootout. A few things have changed. The old Matewan National Bank is now the site of a West Virginia Mine Wars Museum that for the past several years has worked tirelessly to preserve the memory of that important chapter in America's labor history and to honor the sacrifices made by the working men and women of West Virginia, who fought to ensure that the state motto had meaning for all of its citizens.

Montani semper liberi. "Mountaineers Are Always Free."

The March 1912 issue of the magazine *Popular Mechanics* published a short article with the headline "Remarkable Weather of 1911: The Effect of the Combustion of Coal on the Climate—What Scientists Predict for the Future."

The story, little more than a caption on a pencil drawing of a coal-burning factory, said this: "The furnaces of the world are now burning about 2,000,000,000 tons of coal a year. When this is burned, uniting with oxygen, it adds about 7,000,000,000 tons of carbon dioxide to the atmosphere yearly. This tends to make the air a more effective blanket for the earth and to raise its temperature. The effect may be considerable in a few centuries."

To many at the time it may have sounded like science fiction, but the prediction was all too accurate, though it took less than a few centuries for us to see, and suffer, the environmental effects of all that coal. And it hasn't slowed down. In 2021, the world burned more than four times the amount it had burned a hundred years earlier. Coal, the fuel source that drove the Industrial Revolution, that made rail travel possible, that created the steel industry, that was the principal means for heating homes well into the twentieth century, that still provides more than 20 percent of our energy, that in so many ways built the modern world, is the single largest source of global carbon emissions both historically and today—the single largest contributor to global warming.

The United States, indeed most of the industrial world, has been slowly—much too slowly—phasing out coal over the past several decades, and at present we get as much energy from renewable sources such as wind and solar as we do from coal. They still mine it in the mountains of West Virginia, though less and less all the time, and with fewer and fewer workers left in the industry. Their numbers have been dwindling ever since the 1950s when the coal companies switched over from underground mining to strip-mining and mountaintop removal— extraction methods that are safer for miners, but significantly more destructive to the environment.

Over time, mechanization cost most of the miners their jobs. Falling demand contributed, too, as other, cheaper energy replaced coal as the principal power sources for the American

An aerial photo of the ravages of mountaintop removal coal mining in West Virginia.

economy. In the 1950s, there were still 100,000 coal miners working in West Virginia. By the 1980s fewer than half that many still had jobs in the mines. Today the number of coal miners in West Virginia is 12,000, only one out of every four of whom is a card-carrying member of the UMWA.

When the last of those workers loads the last shipment of coal on the last coal train out of West Virginia, it won't be a minute too soon for the environment, but the challenge will remain of finding jobs for those left behind—a challenge that's been deviling the Mountain State for years now as the industry has imploded.

There will be some jobs,

This Environmental Protection Agency map shows the abandoned coal mine areas in West Virginia.

potentially tens of thousands, in reclamation projects on the thousands of abandoned coal mines and hundreds of scarred and gashed coal mountains—one of which, despite years of activism by preservationists, is historic Blair Mountain in Logan County.

Ironically, at a number of old mining sites, alternative energy companies are putting in solar farms, providing yet another source of jobs for the coal miners of the Mountain State.

This abandoned power plant and coal ash landfill on the border of West Virginia and Maryland will see new life as a solar farm.

There's even a US Department of Energy pilot project that could become an industry unto itself to simultaneously clean up toxic acid mine drainage from abandoned mines—chemical contamination that has destroyed many of West Virginia's creeks and rivers—and extract from it critically needed minerals and rare-earth elements essential for much of our technology.

It won't be easy making the transition from a coal economy to whatever comes next—better, safer, environmentally sustainable. Corporate America has successfully lobbied for years to pass so-called right-to-work laws crippling the union movement; workers today have less collective power than at any time since before Roosevelt's New Deal. But no one who knows the proud history of West Virginia's miners, no one who has studied their relentless fight for their rights as workers and as Americans, is likely to doubt that they'll be up for the job.

ACKNOWLEDGMENTS

Many thanks to everyone at Bloomsbury Publishing who helped bring *The Mine Wars* to life: my editor Megan Abbate and designer John Candell, plus Creative Director Donna Mark, Production Editor Oona Patrick, Managing Editor Laura Phillips, Production Manager Nicholas Church, Editorial Director Sarah Shumway, Senior Marketing Director Erica Barmash, Publicity Manager Alexa Higbee, School and Library Marketing team members Beth Eller and Kathleen Morandini, copyeditor Jeff Curry, proofreader Sandra Smith, and Bloomsbury Publisher Mary Kate Castellani. Thanks also to my wife, Janet Watkins, and to the always wonderful Kelly Sonnack at the Andrea Brown Literary Agency. And a special thanks to the late Adrienne Vaughan, president of Bloomsbury USA, with sadness at her passing and continuing prayers for her family.

I owe an enormous debt of gratitude as well to the authors of the dozens of primary and secondary works listed under Sources, most especially James Green for *The Devil Is Here in These Hills*, Robert Shogan for *The Battle of Blair Mountain*, Lon Savage for *Thunder in the Mountains*, Howard Lee for *Bloodletting in Appalachia*, and Elliott Gorn for *Mother Jones: The Most Dangerous Woman in America*, all of whose books

206 - THE MINE WARS

should be required reading in any classes on labor in America and the history of West Virginia. Several people helped us procure photographs for the book, including Lemley Mullett at the West Virginia and Regional History Center, Stan Bumgardner at the West Virginia Humanities Council, Shaun Slifer at the West Virginia Mine Wars Museum, Becky Kauffman at the Eastern Regional Coal Archives, and Aaron Parsons at the West Virginia State Archives. They and their organizations are doing tremendous work to preserve this important history. For anyone who wants to know more about the coal mine wars, the terrific West Virginia Mine Wars Museum in Matewan, West Virginia is an essential resource. You can find out more about the museum at https://wvminewars.org/.

SOURCES

Adams, Mason. "Appalachia's 'Gunmen of Capitalism' and the Matewan Massacre." West Virginia Public Broadcasting, April 19, 2021. https://www.wvpublic.org/section/arts-culture/2021-04-19 /appalachias-gunmen-of-capitalism-and-the-matewan -massacre.

Archer, William. "From Matewan to Welch: One Man's Thirst for Vengeance." *Appalachian Heritage* 20, no. 2 (1992): 9–15.

Bailey, Rebecca. *Matewan before the Massacre: Politics, Coal and the Roots of Conflict in a West Virginia Mining Community.* Morgantown, WV: West Virginia University Press, 2008.

Bartoletti, Susan Campbell. *Growing Up in Coal Country.* Boston: Houghton Mifflin, 1996.

Blizzard, William C. *When Miners March.* Oakland, CA: PM Press, 2010.

Boissoneault, Lorraine. "The Coal Mining Massacre America Forgot." *Smithsonian Magazine*, April 25, 2017. https://www.smithsonianmag.com/history/forgotten-matewan -massacre-was-epicenter-20th-century-mine-wars -180963026/.

Carnegie, Andrew. *The Gospel of Wealth.* New York: Carnegie Corporation of New York, 2017.

"Coal Power's Sharp Rebound Is Taking It to a New Record in 2021, Threatening Net Zero Goals." IEA (International Energy Agency), December 17, 2021. https://www.iea.org/news/coal-power-s-sharp -rebound-is-taking-it-to-a-new-record-in-2021-threatening-net -zero-goals.

Cole, Merle. "Soldiers of the New Empire: The Gaujot Brothers of Mingo County." *West Virginia Historical Society Quarterly* 16, no. 3 (July 2002). https://archive.wvculture.org/history/wvhs /wvhs1603.html.

Conley, Phil M. *Life in a West Virginia Coal Field*. Charleston, WV: American Constitutional Association, 1923.

Corbin, David Alan, ed. *Gun Thugs, Rednecks, and Radicals: A Documentary History of the West Virginia Mine Wars*. Oakland, CA: PM Press, 2011.

Corbin, David Alan. *Life, Work, and Rebellion in the Coal Fields: The Southern West Virginia Miners, 1880–1922*. Urbana, IL: University of Illinois Press, 1981.

Frese, Barbara. *Coal: A Human History*. Cambridge, MA: Perseus Publishing, 2003.

Gorn, Elliot. *Mother Jones: The Most Dangerous Woman in America*. New York: Hill and Wang, 2001.

Green, James. *The Devil Is Here in These Hills: West Virginia's Coal Miners and Their Battle for Freedom*. New York: Grove Press, 2015.

Green, James. "The Price of Life." *Jacobin*, April 21, 2016. https:// jacobin.com/2016/04/massey-blankenship-indictment-coal -appalachia/.

Griswold, Eliza. "Could Coal Waste Be Used to Make Sustainable Batteries?" *New Yorker*, August 26, 2022. https://www.newyorker .com/news/us-journal/could-coal-waste-be-used-to-make-sustainable -batteries.

"A Guide to the Edward L. Stone/Borderland Coal Company Papers." University of Virginia Library Special Collections. https:// ead.lib.virginia.edu/vivaxtf/view?docId=uva-sc/viu00663.xml.

Guilford, Gwynn. "The 100-Year Capitalist Experiment that Keeps Appalachia Poor, Sick, and Stuck on Coal." *Quartz*, December 30, 2017. https://qz.com/1167671/the-100-year-capitalist-experiment -that-keeps-appalachia-poor-sick-and-stuck-on-coal.

"Guns of the Battle of Blair Mountain." *American Rifleman*, March 13, 2014. https://www.americanrifleman.org/content/guns-of-the -battle-of-blair-mountain/.

"Guns, Thugs, and Heros [sic]." *The Roanoker*, July 1979. https:// theroanoker.com/interests/history/coalmining-war.

Hardesty, Ryan, ed. *Better World: Testimony to Congress on the Matewan Massacre: 1920/1921*. Homespun Press, 2018.

Hennen, John. *The Americanization of West Virginia: Creating a Modern Industrial State, 1916–1925*. Lexington, KY: The University Press of Kentucky, 1996.

Hickok, Lorena. *The Reluctant First Lady*. New York: Dodd, Meade, and Company, 1962.

Hochschild, Adam. *American Midnight: The Great War, a Violent Peace, and Democracy's Forgotten Crisis*. New York: HarperCollins /Mariner Books, 2022.

Jones, Mother (Mary Harris Jones). *The Autobiography of Mother Jones*. Chicago: Charles H. Kerr and Company, 1925.

Keeney, Charles Belmont III. "A Union Man: The Life of C. Frank Keeney." *Theses, Dissertations and Capstones*, 2000. https://mds .marshall.edu/cgi/viewcontent.cgi?article=1914&context=etd.

Kelly, Kim. *Fight like Hell: The Untold History of American Labor*. New York: One Signal Publishers/Atria Books, 2022.

Lane, Winthrop D. *Civil War in West Virginia*. New York: B.W. Huebsch, 1921.

Lee, Howard B. *Bloodletting in Appalachia: The Story of West Virginia's Four Major Mine Wars and Other Thrilling Incidents on Its Coal Fields*. Morgantown, WV: West Virginia University Press, 1969.

Lewis, Ronald L. *Black Coal Miners in America: Race, Class, and Community Conflict, 1780–1980*. Lexington, KY: University Press of Kentucky, 1987.

McAteer, Davitt. *Monongah: The Tragic Story of the 1907 Monongah Mine Disaster*. Morgantown, WV: West Virginia University Press, 2014.

Meador, Michael. "The Red Neck War of 1921: The Miners' March and the Battle of Blair Mountain." In *The Goldenseal Book of the West Virginia Mine Wars*, edited by Ken Sullivan, 57–63. Charleston, WV: Goldenseal Magazine, 1991.

Meador, Michael. "The Siege of Crooked Creek Gap." In *The Goldenseal Book of the West Virginia Mine Wars*, edited by Ken Sullivan, 66–72. Charleston, WV: Goldenseal Magazine, 1991.

The Mine Wars: The Desire for Dignity Runs Deep. Directed by Randall MacLowry. PBS American Experience, 2019.

Mistich, Dave. "UMWA Grapples with Coal's Decline, an Uncertain Future." West Virginia Public Broadcasting, September 14, 2021. https://www.wvpublic.org/economy/2021-09-14/umwa-grapples-wit -coals-decline-an-uncertain-future.

Molena, Francis. "Remarkable Weather of 1911." *Popular Mechanics*, March 1912. https://www.snopes.com/fact-check/1912 -article-global-warming/.

Mooney, Fred. *Struggle in the Coal Fields: The Autobiography of Fred Mooney*. Morgantown, WV: West Virginia University Library, 1967.

Mullins, Nick. "West Virginia Coal Mining's Dark Past." *Anthony Bourdain Parts Unknown*. CNN.com, April 26, 2018. https://explorepartsunknown.com/west-virginia/coal-minings-dark-past/.

Murray, Robert. *Red Scare: A Study in National Hysteria, 1919–1920*. University of Minnesota Press, 1955.

"The Primitive Mountaineer." *New York Times*, August 3, 1921.

Robertson, Campbell. "A Century Ago, Miners Fought in a Bloody Uprising. Few Know about It Today." *New York Times*, September 6, 2021. https://www.nytimes.com/2021/09/06/us/coal-miners-blair-mountain.html.

Savage, Joe. "Stopping the Armed March: The Nonunion Resistance." In *The Goldenseal Book of the West Virginia Mine Wars*, edited by Ken Sullivan, 73–79. Charleston, WV: Goldenseal Magazine, 1991.

Savage, Lon. "The Gunfight at Matewan: An Anniversary Speech." In *The Goldenseal Book of the West Virginia Mine Wars*, edited by Ken Sullivan, 45–48. Charleston, WV: Goldenseal Magazine, 1991.

Savage, Lon. *Thunder in the Mountains: The West Virginia Mine War 1920–21*. Pittsburgh: University of Pittsburgh Press, 1990.

Settle, Mary Lee. *Addie: A Memoir*. Columbia, SC: University of South Carolina Press, 1998.

Sherwood, Topper. "The Dust Settles: Felts Papers Offer More on Matewan." In *The Goldenseal Book of the West Virginia Mine Wars*, edited by Ken Sullivan, 51–55. Charleston, WV: Goldenseal Magazine, 1991.

Shogan, Robert. *The Battle of Blair Mountain: The Story of America's Largest Labor Uprising*. New York: Basic Books, 2004.

"Sid Hatfield Slain before Court House." *New York Times*, August 2, 1921.

Spargo, John. *The Bitter Cry of Children*. New York: Macmillan, 1906.

Spivak, John L. *A Man in His Time*. New York: Horizon Press, 1967.

Stein, Jeff. "West Virginia Coal Country Will Test Power of Democrats' Climate Bill." *Washington Post*, August 13, 2022. https://www.washingtonpost.com/us-policy/2022/08/13/inflation-reduction-act-west-virginia/.

Sullivan, Ken, ed. *The Goldenseal Book of the West Virginia Mine Wars*. Charleston, WV: Goldenseal Magazine, 1991.

Swick, Gerald. *Historic Photos of West Virginia*. Nashville: Turner Publishing Company, 2010.

Towers, George. "West Virginia's Lost Youth: Appalachian Stereotypes and Residential Preferences." *Journal of Geography* 104, no. 2 (March 2005): 74–84.

United States Senate Committee on Education and Labor. West Virginia Coal Fields: Hearings before the Committee on Education and Labor. 67th Cong., 1921.

"Warren G. Harding." *TheWhiteHouse.gov*. https://www.whitehouse.gov/about-the-white-house/presidents/warren-g-harding/.

Yoho, R.G. *The Nine Lives of Charles E. Lively: The Deadliest Man in the West Virginia–Colorado Coal Mine Wars*. Burlington, NC: Fox Run Publishing, 2020.

PHOTO CREDITS

ii-iii: Lewis Wickes Hine/Library of Congress; **ix:** Heidi Perov/West Virginia Encyclopedia and West Virginia Humanities Council; **2:** Eastern Regional Coal Archives; **5:** Mooney collection/West Virginia and Regional History Center, West Virginia University Libraries; **7:** Lee collection/West Virginia and Regional History Center, West Virginia University Libraries; **12:** West Virginia and Regional History Center, West Virginia University Libraries; **15:** Library of Congress; **16: (top)** West Virginia and Regional History Center, West Virginia University Libraries; **(bottom)** collection of Kenneth King/West Virginia Mine Wars Museum; **17:** collection of Kenneth King/West Virginia Mine Wars Museum; **19:** William O. Trevey Glass Slide Collection/Archives & Special Collections, McConnell Library, Radford University; **21:** West Virginia and Regional History Center, West Virginia University Libraries; **22:** Lewis Wickes Hine/West Virginia and Regional History Center, West Virginia University Libraries; **24:** National Child Labor Committee, Washington, D.C./West Virginia and Regional History Center, West Virginia University Libraries; **27:** West Virginia and Regional History Center, West Virginia University Libraries; **30:** Vaughn L. Kiger/West Virginia and Regional History Center, West Virginia University Libraries; **32:** Bittner collection/West Virginia and Regional History Center, West Virginia University Libraries; **34:** Harris & Ewing/Library of Congress; **38:** West Virginia State Archives; **39:** West Virginia and Regional History Center, West Virginia University Libraries; **42:** Coal Life collection/West Virginia State Archives; **40:** Jack Testerman via Ginny Savage Ayers; **49:** Lee collection/West Virginia and Regional History Center, West Virginia University Libraries; **54:** Coal Life collection/West Virginia State Archives; **56:** Richard Duez/West Virginia and Regional History Center, West Virginia University Libraries; **58:** Susan H. Maxwell/West Virginia and Regional History Center, West Virginia University Libraries; **60:** Lee collection/West Virginia and Regional History Center, West Virginia University Libraries; **62:** Michael Workman/West Virginia and Regional History Center, West Virginia University Libraries; **66:** West Virginia and Regional History Center, West Virginia University Libraries; **67: (top)** Robert Y. Spence/e-WV: The West Virginia Encyclopedia;

(bottom) Mooney collection/West Virginia and Regional History Center, West Virginia University Libraries; **74:** Lee collection/West Virginia and Regional History Center, West Virginia University Libraries; **77:** Bittner collection/West Virginia and Regional History Center, West Virginia University Libraries; **79:** Bittner collection/West Virginia and Regional History Center, West Virginia University Libraries; **83:** Lee collection/West Virginia and Regional History Center, West Virginia University Libraries; **85:** *Huntington Advertiser*, June 2, 1920/West Virginia Encyclopedia; **95:** Lee collection/West Virginia and Regional History Center, West Virginia University Libraries; **101:** Pocahontas Operators' Association/West Virginia and Regional History Center, West Virginia University Libraries; **103:** Wikimedia Commons; **112:** Upstateherd/Wikimedia Commons; **117:** Harris & Ewing/West Virginia and Regional History Center, West Virginia University Libraries; **121:** *The Wheeling Intelligencer*, August 2, 1921/ Chronicling America at the Library of Congress; **130:** *National Geographic/* West Virginia and Regional History Center, West Virginia University Libraries; **137:** *Martinsburg Journal*, August 25, 1921/Chronicling America at the Library of Congress; **141:** William C. and Bill Blizzard "When Miners March" Coal and Labor Collection, Appalachian Collection, McConnell Library, Radford University; **143:** Moffett, Chicago/Library of Congress; **147:** *National Geographic/*West Virginia and Regional History Center, West Virginia University Libraries; **153:** Sara Jane Pollock/West Virginia and Regional History Center, West Virginia University Libraries; **154:** *The West Virginian*, August 31, 1921/Chronicling America at the Library of Congress; **162:** Lee collection/West Virginia and Regional History Center, West Virginia University Libraries; **166:** West Virginia State Archives; **169:** Boardman Robinson, published in *The Liberator*, October 1921/ Library of Congress; **170:** Wikimedia Commons; **171:** West Virginia State Archives; **173:** Wikimedia Commons; **174:** West Virginia State Archives; **178:** Mooney collection/West Virginia and Regional History Center, West Virginia University Libraries; **180:** West Virginia and Regional History Center, West Virginia University Libraries; **183:** National Photo Company Collection/Library of Congress; **185:** Bettmann Archive/Getty Images; **190:** U.S. Army Corps of Engineers Digital Library; **194:** published by American Constitutional Association, Charleston, West Virginia, 1923; **199:** West Virginia and Regional History Center, West Virginia University Libraries; **202: (top)** Andrew Lichtenstein/Corbis/Getty Images; **(bottom)** developed by SRA International for the U.S. Environmental Protection Agency; **203:** Acroterion/Wikimedia Commons

ENDNOTES

4   "that unless he gets rid of": Gorn, *Mother Jones*, 174.

6   "Why did they shoot me?": Shogan, *The Battle of Blair Mountain*, 25.

6   "Split the creek": Shogan, *The Battle of Blair Mountain*, 25.

8   "Them sons of bitches had it comin'": Savage, *Thunder in the Mountains*, 25.

13   "There seems to be": McAteer, *Monongha*, 190.

14   "I 'led the sheet'": Mooney, *Struggle in the Coal Fields*, 10.

15   "We don't seem to be getting anywhere": Mooney, *Struggle in the Coal Fields*, 10.

15   "human drift": Mooney, *Struggle in the Coal Fields*, 12.

17   "We work in *his* plant": Corbin, *Gun Thugs, Rednecks, and Radicals*, 18.

23   "I met one little fellow": Spargo, *The Bitter Cry of Children*, 165.

28   "Most of the miners' houses were pathetic": Settle, *Addie*, 96.

30   "judicious mixture": Lewis, *Black Coal Miners in America*, 121.

35   "our boys would have dropped": Savage, *Thunder in the Mountains*, 26.

36   "They wore 'coats o' nails'": Mooney, *Struggle in the Coal Fields*, 70.

36   "Dear Tom": Sherwood, "The Dust Settles," 51.

36   "It is generally talked": Sherwood, "The Dust Settles," 51.

37   "Reese [sic] Chambers": Sherwood, "The Dust Settles," 51.

37   "the consensus [sic] of opinion": Sherwood, "The Dust Settles," 54.

39   "You have stood": Savage, *Thunder in the Mountains*, 28–29.

40   "Medieval West Virginia": Jones, *The Autobiography of Mother Jones*, 234–235.

40   "With its tent colonies": Jones, *The Autobiography of Mother Jones*, 235.

41   "Get it straight": Gorn, *Mother Jones*, 3.

45   "a good pummeling": Shogan, *The Battle of Blair Mountain*, 15.

47   "Hatfield shot Testerman": Shogan, *The Battle of Blair Mountain*, 89.

48   "Felts shot from the hip": Shogan, *The Battle of Blair Mountain*, 90.

49   "a little shooting match": Savage, *Thunder in the Mountains*, 13.

53   "I gave him a book": Green, *The Devil Is Here in These Hills*, 55.

54   "Here the miners had been peons": Jones, *The Autobiography of Mother Jones*, 148.

57   "a regular hurricane of bullets": Green, *The Devil Is Here in These Hills*, 95.

58   "God does not walk in these hills": Green, *The Devil Is Here in These Hills*, 96.

60   "So brothers you can call [us]": Corbin, *Life, Work and Rebellion in the Coal Fields*.

61   "This is the first time": Lee, *Bloodletting in Appalachia*, 29.

63   "Whatever I have done": Gorn, *Mother Jones*, 188.

63   "I can raise just as much hell": Gorn, *Mother Jones*, 189.

68   "Standing Army of Logan": Shogan, *The Battle of Blair Mountain*, 172.

69   "I'm sorry to hear you say that, Don": Spivak, *A Man in His Time*, 58–59.

70   "We'll kill those sons of bitches": Shogan, *The Battle of Blair Mountain*, 95.

71   "No local union": Green, *The Devil Is Here in These Hills*, 33.

71   "Shut up": Hardesty, *Better World*, 52.

71   "The only message you can get out": Hardesty, *Better World*, 52.

71   "I want to carry you down the road": Hardesty, *Better World*, 53.

75   "I know how a scab is made up": Gorn, *Mother Jones*, 173.

77   "Huddled under canvas": Shogan, *The Battle of Blair Mountain*, 81–82.

78   "Inside, on a 'cot'": Savage, *Thunder in the Mountains*, 40.

78   "no act of God": Bailey, *Matewan Before the Massacre*, 225.

79   "The Socialist or Anarchist who seeks": Carnegie, *The Gospel of Wealth*.

81 "The miners and their families": Yoho, *The Nine Lives of Charles E. Lively*, 68.

85 "It means no more to me": Yoho, *The Nine Lives of Charles E. Lively*, 80.

86 "I reckon you thought I had horns": Savage, *Thunder in the Mountains*, 43.

86 "just a little free-for-all": Shogan, *The Battle of Blair Mountain*, 93.

86 "It was a question of life or death": Savage, *Thunder in the Mountains*, 43.

86 "go out and kill the last damned one of them": Shogan, *The Battle of Blair Mountain*, 96.

86 "I would be did": Shogan, *The Battle of Blair Mountain*, 97.

87 "We'll kill those sons of bitches": Shogan, *The Battle of Blair Mountain*, 105.

87 "Let's kill every damn one of them": Shogan, *The Battle of Blair Mountain*, 98–99.

88 "A slight man of medium build": Spivak, *A Man in His Time*, 91.

88 "Lively and I were born and reared": Mooney, *Struggle in the Coal Fields*, 72.

89 "C.E. seemed to think": Blizzard, *When Miners March*, 386.

92 "Did Sid Hatfield make any statement": Savage, *Thunder in the Mountains*, 45–46.

93 "They still tell how the jury": Savage, *Thunder in the Mountains*, 48–49.

94 "It's the happiest day": Savage, *Thunder in the Mountains*, 49.

98 "a shooting bee": Shogan, *The Battle of Blair Mountain*, 117.

101 "The big advantage of this martial law": Green, *The Devil Is Here in These Hills*, 231.

104 "an organized band of robbers": Hardesty, *Better World*, 23–25.

105 "We have tried every possible way": Hardesty, *Better World*, 20.

106 "I say we have the same right": Shogan, *The Battle of Blair Mountain*, 141.

106 "I can explain it this way": Shogan, *The Battle of Blair Mountain*, 141–142.

107 "I went up and told Mr. Felts": U.S. Senate, Sid Hatfield.

107 "Then the shooting started in general": U.S. Senate, Sid Hatfield.

108 "This is the first I heard of it": U.S. Senate, Sid Hatfield.

108 "At the same time, while you were accepting money": U.S. Senate, Charlie Lively.

112 "There is Mr. Lively": U.S. Senate, Jessie Hatfield.

113 "Kill 'em with one gun": Lee, *Bloodletting in Appalachia*, 68.

113 "He was poor protection": U.S. Senate, Jessie Hatfield.

114 "My husband, he rolled back down the steps": U.S. Senate, Sallie Chambers.

114 "Oh, please, Mr. Lively, don't shoot him anymore": U.S. Senate, Sallie Chambers.

115 "What did you do this for?": U.S. Senate, Sallie Chambers.

115 "One of the guns": "Sid Hatfield Slain," *New York Times*, 1.

116 "I happened to look down the steps": Yoho, *The Nine Lives of Charles E. Lively*, 110.

117 "We have gathered here today": Mooney, *Struggle in the Coal Fields*, 89.

118 "My work is my love": Yoho, *The Nine Lives of Charles E. Lively*, 74.

120 "Never in the history of the country": Green, *The Devil Is Here in These Hills*, 250.

120 "the most glaring and outrageous expression": Shogan, *The Battle of Blair Mountain*, 162.

120 "Those who saw the bodies": Yoho, *The Nine Lives of Charles E. Lively*, 100.

122 "When Hatfield and Chambers went": Yoho, *The Nine Lives of Charles E. Lively*, 109.

122 "Hatfields and McCoys are as famous": "The Primitive Mountaineer," *New York Times*.

125 "Therefore, you have no recourse": Lee, *Bloodletting in Appalachia*, 96.

126 "a tool of the [expletive] coal operators": Lee, *Bloodletting in Appalachia*, 96.

128 "red-soaked in the doctrines of Bolshevism": Murray, *Red Scare*, 156.

130 "The boys need guns, etc.": Green, *The Devil Is Here in These Hills*, 252.

131 "Don, you can pistol whip them if you want": Green, *The Devil Is Here in These Hills*, 184.

131 "It looked more like Dante's Inferno": Blizzard, *When Miners March*, 103.

133 "I wash my hands of the whole affair": Shogan, *The Battle of Blair Mountain*, 167.

134 "moonshine liquor": Green, *The Devil Is Here in These Hills*, 257.

134 "We'll hang Don Chafin": Shogan, *The Battle of Blair Mountain*, 190.

134 "Standing Army of Logan": Shogan, *The Battle of Blair Mountain*, 173.

135 "No armed mob will cross Logan County": Savage, *Thunder in the Mountains*, 81.

136 "I request that you abandon your purpose": Savage, *Thunder in the Mountains*, 78.

137 "an army of pompous phrases": "Warren G. Harding."

138 "Less government in business": "Warren G. Harding."

138 "'Well boys,' he said, 'that telegram is a fake'": Green, *The Devil Is Here in These Hills*, 259.

142 "Where are you going?": Shogan, *The Battle of Blair Mountain*, 194.

142 "army of malcontents": Shogan, *The Battle of Blair Mountain*, 174.

144 "Gas. You understand" Green, *The Devil Is Here in These Hills*, 266.

144 "You two are the officers": Mooney, *Struggle in the Coal Fields*, 92.

146 "I've told you men": Corbin, *Life, Work, and Rebellion*, 223–224.

148 A regular son of a bitch he was": Green, *The Devil Is Here in These Hills*, 267.

148 "What the hell you fellows mean": Mooney, *Struggle in the Coal Fields*, 99.

150 "Who are you?": Shogan, *The Battle of Blair Mountain*, 186–187.

152 "a monster powder keg": Savage, *Thunder in the Mountains*, 111.

153 "national stench and disgrace": Green, *The Devil Is Here in These Hills*, 271.

153 "Danger of attack": Shogan, *The Battle of Blair Mountain*, 191.

154 "Whereas the Governor of West Virginia": Savage, *Thunder in the Mountains*, 121.

154 "Therefore, I, Warren G. Harding": Savage, *Thunder in the Mountains*, 112–113.

155 "It is believed that the withdrawal": Shogan, *The Battle of Blair Mountain*, 200.

156 "Come on boys": Savage, *Thunder in the Mountains*, 123.

162 "Two boys was killed": Green, *The Devil Is Here in These Hills*, 274.

163 "Unless troops sent by midnight": Green, *The Devil Is Here in These Hills*, 275.

164 "Someone spies the dark shadow": Savage, *Thunder in the Mountains*, 128.

170 "The idea, in fact, was totally unthinkable": Savage, *Thunder in the Mountains*, 147.

171 "PLANES DROP BOMBS": Green, *The Devil Is Here in These Hills*, 280.

172 "Are you the general": Savage, *Thunder in the Mountains*, 150.

172 "Does this mean you are going to allow": Savage, *Thunder in the Mountains*, 150.

174 "That's why you don't see the guns": Savage, *Thunder in the Mountains*, 150–151.

174 "so unmistakably under the influence": Savage, *Thunder in the Mountains*, 153.

174 "that there had been dissension": Savage, *Thunder in the Mountains*, 154.

179 "We see no reason for charging": Corbin, *Life, Work, and Rebellion*, 237.

179 "Whatever their offenses": Corbin, *Life, Work, and Rebellion*, 237.

179 "These men aided, abetted": Corbin, *Life, Work, and Rebellion*, 238.

179 "A lot of people will tell you": Savage, *Thunder in the Mountains*, 136.

181 "William Blizzard, right field, treason": Green, *The Devil Is Here in These Hills*, 297.

181 "By a jury of his peers": Green, *The Devil Is Here in These Hills*, 299–300.

183 "I'd rather be in hell": Shogan, *The Battle of Blair Mountain*, 218.

184 "Scott's Run, a coal-mining community": Hickok, *The Reluctant First Lady*, 137–138.

186 "Employers want to measure wages": Corbin, *Life, Work, and Rebellion*, 245.

186 "Imagine 23,000 coal miners": Mooney, *Struggle in the Coal Fields*, 59–60.

188 "I've done the best I could": Gorn, *Mother Jones*, 292.

188 "All the demons in hell": Green, *The Devil Is Here in These Hills*, 328.

189 "hallowed ground": Savage, "The Gunfight at Matewan," 45–46.

191 "During a dozen years": Corbin, *Gun Thugs, Rednecks, and Radicals*, 1–2.

191 "When we were told of the importance": Corbin, *Gun Thugs, Rednecks, and Radicals*, 1–2.

192 "Leavers": Towers, "West Virginia's Lost Youth," 74–84.

193 "No man worthy of the name": Lee, *Bloodletting in Appalachia*, 22–24.

194 "respect for the constitutional authorities": Hennen, *The Americanization of West Virginia*, 97

198 "My dear friends": Gorn, *Mother Jones*, 293.

200 "The furnaces of the world": Molena, "Remarkable Weather of 1911."

INDEX